KNOCKED

DOWN

BUT NOT

DESTROYED

AN AUTOBIOGRAPHY

KNOCKED

DOWN

BUT NOT

DESTROYED

GREGG E. GRIFFITHS

Pleasant Word

A Division of WinePress Group

Pleasant Word (a division of WinePress Publishing, PO Box 428, Enumclaw, WA 98022) functions only as book publisher. As such, the ultimate design, content, editorial accuracy, and views expressed or implied in this work are those of the author.

Unless otherwise noted, all Scriptures are taken from the *Holy Bible, New International Version*®, *NIV*®. Copyright © 1973, 1978, 1984 by Biblica, Inc.™ Used by permission of Zondervan. All rights reserved worldwide. WWW. ZONDERVAN.COM

Scripture references marked KJV are taken from the *King James Version* of the Bible.

Scripture references marked NASB are taken from the *New American Standard Bible*, © 1960, 1963, 1968, 1971, 1972, 1973, 1975, 1977 by The Lockman Foundation. Used by permission.

ISBN 13: 978-1-4141-1600-6
ISBN 10: 1-4141-1600-4
Library of Congress Catalog Card Number: 2009909166

This book is dedicated to my daughters Erica, Amy, and Danna. It was through their prodding that this book became a reality. To all my grandchildren — your mothers said you needed to know what Ompa had accomplished. They believed they knew the stories. They did live some of them with me, but they are learning more of what their dad has really done.

CONTENTS

Acknowledgments ix
Introduction. xi

Chapter One: Military Experience 1
Chapter Two: Law Enforcement. 27
Chapter Three: Conversion Experience and the Bestowment
       of Gifts. 37
Chapter Four: A Brief Overview of the Gifts 43
Chapter Five: Gifts of Revelation 47
Chapter Six : Gifts of Inspiration 67
Chapter Seven: Gifts of Power 73
Chapter Eight: Post Script 107
Chapter Nine: How to Obtain This Power. 115

Endnotes 119

ACKNOWLEDGMENTS

FIRST OF ALL, I want to publicly thank God for His wonderful love, mercy, and care for me. Had it not been for His grace and mercy, I would be dead, and this book would never have been written.

Next, I want to thank my daughters for their coaching, prodding, suggesting, etc. Thanks, girls!

Many thanks to all the friends who contributed to this book.

Thanks to Michael O'Loughlin, who contributed a story which I had totally forgotten.

Thanks to my beloved sister-in-law, Karen, whose questions I tried to answer in the book and whose knowledge of grammar and structure made all of this much easier.

Thank you to my brother-in-law, Fredrick Francis, who gave me a lot of help through revisions upon revisions.

Thank you to my grandson Jered, for his help with the photos

And finally, a special thank you to my wife, for putting up with me during this project.

INTRODUCTION

IT IS AN awesome thought knowing we are in the presence of the Lord each day. Have you ever wondered what it would be like to be used by God in a miraculous way? Have you ever pondered why the power displayed in the Old Testament and the miracles Jesus and His apostles performed in the New Testament aren't happening that way today? We have sung songs about the "wonder working power," and we have heard stories about people being healed, rising from the dead, and even controlling the weather. When I committed my life to Jesus Christ, the Bible came alive not only in my life but in the lives of those around me. It is awesome realizing that we are daily in the presence of the living God. The Old Testament prophet Isaiah realized this when he answered God's call:

> Then I said, Woe is me, for I am ruined! Because I am a man of unclean lips, And I live among a people of unclean lips; For my eyes have seen the King, the Lord of hosts.
>
> —Isaiah 6:5 (NASB)

Simon Peter realized he was in the presence of the Holy One when, after he and his colleagues had been fishing all night without success, Jesus instructed them to let down their nets on the other side of the boat. According to the account in the gospel of Luke 5:6-8, they let down their nets on the other side of the boat and the catch was so great, it nearly sank both boats.

> But when Simon Peter saw that, he fell down at Jesus' feet, saying, . . . Depart from me, for I am a sinful man, O Lord!
>
> —Luke 5:8 (NASB)

Over the years I have been asked to teach the Bible to young adults, senior citizens, and even children. I love to talk about the Lord, and some tell me I become very excited when I do. That is because God has done many exciting things in my life. As I teach, many experiences from my military days come to the fore as examples, and this includes my Vietnam experiences. The same is true of experiences during my law enforcement days. No one's experiences, including mine, prove the Bible; rather, the Bible proves or gives credence to my experiences.

This book is not about me but about how the Lord has used me for His glory and honor to help strike blows for His Kingdom. This is not intended to be a scholarly work, but is written to be an encouragement to those really wanting to be used by the Holy Spirit to see Scripture come alive in their everyday living experience.

In 1995, The Barna Group did a survey on spiritual gifts with the following results:

- Most people (71%) say they have heard of spiritual gifts.

- Among those who have heard of spiritual gifts, 31% can name a spiritual gift they believe they possess. That is the equivalent of 22% of the total adult public who can identify possessing a spiritual gift.

- 12% of those who have heard of spiritual gifts claim they do not have one.

- The most commonly claimed gifts are teaching (7%), helps/service (7%), faith (4%), knowledge (4%), mercy (4%), and tongues (3%).

This survey shows that many Christians do not have an understanding of the spiritual gifts, do not know how to receive the gifts, and do not realize how spiritual gifts can affect not only their lives but the lives of those around them.

God has brought me through amazing situations through using the gifts of the Holy Spirit. I will share stories of close and heavy combat in Vietnam, police chases, and life-saving situations. I served as a U.S. Army combat medic in Vietnam, with a price on my head put there by the Viet Cong who did not like medics saving American lives. After my service, I returned to the real world and became a police officer, hoping to save lives. I did save lives, but not in the way I originally thought. When I became a Christian, things changed.

Many have suggested over the years that I record my life experiences and the way the Lord has worked through all of it. I have often wondered who would read such a book. Now that I have written it, I suppose I will just wait and see. My daughters encouraged me to put my experiences on paper, if for no other reason than to let my grandchildren know what their grandpa really did. As my daughter Amy put it, "Dad, either you write your book or we girls will. We know a lot of the stories because we lived some of them with you."

The apostle Paul wrote, "...be not drunk with wine, wherein is excess; but be filled with the Spirit" (Ephesians 5:18 KJV). If we are going to follow Christ, we must follow this command and be filled with his Spirit. With that filling comes power. I have many more stories in addition to the ones I am telling in this book, but I have tried to limit myself to those reflecting specifically on the use of the spiritual gifts in everyday living. Many people call this "lifestyle evangelism." These stories cover some thirty years. I wish I could claim these sorts of things happened to me every single day, but not even the apostles could do that.

John Newton's hymn "Amazing Grace" has meant a lot to me over the years. The third verse in particular holds great meaning: "Thro' many dangers, toils, and snares, I have already come; 'Tis grace hath bro't me safe thus far, and grace will lead me home." A Bible verse that sums up my experience with the Lord is Mark 16:20, which says "the disciples spread the Good News everywhere. The Lord worked with them. He confirmed his word by the miraculous signs that accompanied it" (GW). As I have ministered both on and off the job, the Lord has worked through me for his glory. As you read my stories and see how the Lord has worked, I pray that these will cause a desire in you to be used of the Lord in mighty and wonder-filled ways.

I am calling my book *Knocked Down*, and this title comes by way of my life's experiences. I do believe that "we are afflicted in every way, but not crushed; perplexed, but not despairing; persecuted, but not forsaken; struck down, but not destroyed; always carrying about in the body the dying of Jesus, that the life of Jesus also may be manifested in our body" (2 Corinthians 4:8-10 NASB).

CHAPTER ONE

MILITARY EXPERIENCE

I HAVE FOUND that God packs life situations with more than one level of meaning or relevance in His plan for each person. He is at work in manifold ways that are interlinked to accomplish the greatest good not only for the individual's life, but also for those around them.

I was raised a Baptist in a very conservative Baptist General Conference congregation. I grew up in the suburbs of Minneapolis, Minnesota, and graduated from a very strong academic high school. One of my classmates graduated as a presidential scholar. We had a large graduating class of over eight hundred students and I graduated dead center. I spent two years studying music education in a college in southern Minnesota.

Besides attending classes and practicing the piano, I lived and worked in a local hospital's psychiatric ward. I worked the ward and was on call for the rest of the hospital's wards through the night. I was also the secretary for the professional music fraternity, and I tried to have some sort of a social life. I completed three years of college in two calendar years, and by that point I was just about burned out.

The military draft was in full swing at that time, for it was the Vietnam era. If eligibly-aged men weren't in school, chances were very good they would be drafted into military service. Before allowing that to happen, I enlisted in the army, wanting to become an operating-room technician. I went in on the one-hundred-twenty-day delay program, and on the day of induction I was told, "School is closed." What I did not know then was that because I had enlisted for this schooling, and now the army could not provide it, I could have proudly walked away, having completed my military obligation.

The sergeant suggested I look at another opportunity in the medical field. He suggested a course referred to as 91A10 Medical Care and Treatment of the Patient. That sounded like safe hospital work to me. When I asked what this was exactly, he stated he wasn't sure but knew it was in the medical field somewhere. *Yes, I guess it was!* I had enlisted to become a combat medic, the guy out there in the field alongside the infantry soldier. The medic who, according to Bill Cosby, says, "Sorry, I don't make house calls in the heat of battle." Later I was told that the life expectancy of the medic in the middle of combat is about seven seconds. This is where my exciting life outside of faith in Christ started, and even though I know I was way outside of God's will, I can look back and see that I was never out of His care.

God's Care

My first stop was Fort Campbell, Kentucky, to start basic training. Everyone called the first week in the reception station "hell week," and with very good reason. There were tests, injections, and very little sleep. It was a week of being yelled at and getting oriented to the army's way of doing things. Some days actually boggled logic.

I made it through that week and time marched on. Finally, I was assigned to my training unit. I was there for about an hour when I was called out and told to return to the reception station because my records were lost. I was back in the reception station for less than thirty minutes when I was told my records were found, at which time I was going to return to my training unit. But I was also informed that I had already been dropped from the roster of my unit and now needed to spend another week in the reception station! This meant more KP, more yelling, more loss of sleep, and so on. After two more days of this, I told my sergeant I wasn't sure how much more I could take. He gave me some good advice: Learn to laugh at it. So I did. In the end I made it through, but I was now a week behind everyone else.

At the end of my second hell week, I was assigned to a new training unit. The drill instructor's name was Staff Sergeant Love. Love was a tall, slender, black man who was an Airborne Ranger. This man was tough. It seemed when most other units were walking, we were low-crawling. When other units rode to training sites, we ran or marched. He told us he was preparing us for Vietnam, and he was going to give us the basics to survive. And that is what he did. When I went to Nam and actually got into combat, the sergeant's training and the grace of God got me through many rough situations.

Basic training for our unit was out of the box. An example of how far out was when my company was in the field for training. Fall of the year in Kentucky can be rainy and cold. One of the troops forgot to bring his poncho with him that day. It was raining heavily and we were getting drenched. We asked permission of the sergeant to put our ponchos on, but he denied that request. The reason was that because one guy did not bring his poncho, no one else could put on theirs because all would not be uniform. Then he said, "Besides, you are not really getting wet. Your clothes are wet, but your skin repels water, so you really are not wet." I think almost everyone came down with colds after that experience. It was just one more way of breaking us down mentally and causing us to conform to the army way of doing things.

After Fort Campbell, my next stop was Fort Sam Houston, Texas. I got there in the early part of December, 1967, and the weather was much nicer than where I had just been. In fact, I believe on the day I reported for duty the sun was shining. The new training class had formed, and along with about twenty others, I was called out of formation and sent to the Leadership Preparatory School. I was to spend the next two weeks going through the entire ten-week medical training. We wore purple-colored helmet liners and were considered the class leaders. Because of the purple helmet liners, we were referred to as "Grape Heads." We were to become the tutors, drill instructors, and mothers to a lot of personnel we would train when our own leadership training was completed.

In the leadership program, we were awakened at 4:00 A.M. We showered, shaved, had breakfast, and were in the classroom by 6:00 A.M. By 10:00 or 11:00 P.M. we would return to our barracks and then do the rest of the military details, including shining our boots and cleaning the barracks after the drill instructors messed up our beds and scuffed the floor. We were granted two hours of sleep a night, and we were expected to stay awake during our training the next day. Some of the men learned how to sleep standing up.

At the end of our medical training, we were given two weeks off for Christmas and were told to report back just after the New Year to be assigned our new training unit. I was now five weeks behind where I should have been originally.

There were some perks to being a Grape-Head such as our being given "walking passes." That meant that after training we were permitted to leave the base as long as we were back by 4:30 A.M. to wake the trainees up and get the day started.

While on leave, my wife and I got married. I had already set up an off-base apartment so she would have a place to live. With the walking pass, I could be with her in the evenings, but I was back to work in the morning.

While most of my class was sent to Vietnam upon completion of the combat medical training, I was not. Instead, since they had no orders for me, I was told to report to the Receiving and Holding Company (R+H). I heard that the class I originally formed up with at the beginning of December, the one I was called out of, were killed as their plane was rocketed when landing in Vietnam. I figured I just missed my first appointment with death, for I could have been on that plane.

Finally, the orders for Vietnam came. I was to report to McChord Air Force Base for processing to Southeast Asia. I did not tell my wife about the orders right away. There was a military officer living next door to us, so I first talked with him about this. He suggested I take her out, have a fun, relaxing evening, and then break the news to her—gently. I did all of this, but there were still many tears.

If the past six months had not been exciting enough, the next year was going to really test me. I wasn't sure where God was, or if He even existed; nevertheless, over the next year God was going to demonstrate great love for me.

Vietnam

> But God commendeth his love toward us, in that, while we were yet sinners, Christ died for us.
>
> —Romans 5:8 (KJV)

In April of 1968 I arrived in Cam Ran Bay, South Vietnam. The army had another dreaded reception station there, where I spent a week before being assigned to my permanent unit. During that week the troops were oriented to the country, the climate, and what to expect out in the field. Having been trained as a medic, it had been a number of months since I last saw or handled any sort of weapon. I had qualified Expert on the M-14 during basic training, and I had a day of training on the M-16. While in the reception station, I was introduced to the M-60 machine gun, the M-79 grenade launcher, and the LAU, which is a single-use, smaller version of a bazooka. After firing the M-60, the training sergeant said he was going to change my classification of training from combat medic to automatic rifleman. I told him, "No, thank you!"

On about the fourth night in the reception station, we were to go out on an ambush patrol. I was selected to go as the automatic rifleman and not as a medic with the other ten to fifteen men. The sergeant who led the patrol was a small man with beady eyes and a really sour disposition. He informed the squad that if anyone opened fire before he did, he would personally shoot the man who did.

We set up an L-shaped ambush on a path that led to the bay. We were about fifty yards in from the shore, and I was on the leg of the "L" with two other guys. That put us just off the path. At about 2:00 A.M., we saw three Viet Cong walking on the path toward us. We had them sighted in, but because the sergeant had not opened fire, we weren't going to shoot.

Suddenly a flare went off. We ducked down so as not to give away our position. When the flare went out, the three Viet Cong were gone, but there was now a satchel charge sitting about fifteen feet in front of us.

A satchel charge is nothing more than a sandbag filled with explosives, a timer, and a fuse. We could hear it ticking. I started to dig a shallow hole to try and get below the blast should it explode. Another guy from an adjacent position crawled over to our position to make us aware of the bomb sitting in front of us. We were well aware! I was elected to pray. I started with, "Dear God, if you are God. . . ."

It had been a long time since I had prayed, and as I said before, I really had no recent contact with the Lord. Shortly thereafter, we heard the fuse burn, yet the sandbag did not explode. Another flare went up at about 4:00 A.M., and when it died the bomb was gone. Once again God protected me.

The ambush patrol that went out the next night did not fare as well. Over half of those troops were wounded or killed. Some years later, I was speaking to a man who worked with the sergeant who had taken us on our ambush patrol. What I learned was that only Rangers went out on ambush patrols. I was not a Ranger and should not have even been there.

Unit Assignment

At the end of my first week in the reception station, I was sent to the 23rd Medical Battalion in Chu Lai. That's about sixty miles south of Da Nang on the South China Sea. This was Division Headquarters for the Americal Division. The Americal Division was made up of many different units. There were the 196th, 198th, and the 23rd light infantry units, just to name a few. My unit was a field clearing station. The *M.A.S.H* series that played for so long on TV was actually similar to my unit. We would provide personnel re-supply for medics in the field, for dust-off missions, and convoy medics. We also had medical, surgical, and psychiatric wards, as the division psychiatrist was stationed in our unit.

I was awarded two medals during my tour of duty in Vietnam. The first was The Soldiers Medal of Valor, and the second one was the Army Commendation Medal. On July 27, 1968, I was on bunker guard watching the South China Sea. The following details the events not covered in the citation write-up for The Soldiers Medal of Valor.

Three soldiers from the Americal Division Band had gone swimming in the South China Sea. (*Americal* is the correct spelling. It is a combination of American and the New Caledonian Islands in the South Pacific.) One soldier, who subsequently drowned, had taken an inflatable air mattress into the water with him. The mattress was torn open by some coral and filled with water. One of the swimmers made it to the rocky shoreline but was unable to get out of the water. I went to his aid and pulled him out using my M-16. I then took the sling off the weapon and went in after the other two swimmers.

When I reached them, one was unconscious, and the other was holding him up. The unconscious swimmer was still holding on to the now deflated air mattress. The man had a death-grip on that air mattress. I attempted to pry it out of hand, but I could not get his fingers to release it. I told the conscious swimmer to head for shore, because if he got into trouble, there was no way I would be able to help him. He was so exhausted and disoriented that he started to swim out to sea. I grabbed him and turned him toward shore. What I didn't know at the time was that I put him onto a rock.

I then struggled with the other man. I first tried a chin carry, but a wave broke over us and he left my grasp. It was just after sundown, and the waves were high on a very turbulent South China Sea. I surface dove and went under to find him, and when I did, I pushed him up to the surface. He was no longer breathing. I attempted mouth-to-mouth resuscitation, but that was useless because he was too heavy with the air mattress. I thought it would be better to get him on shore and then we could do more to help him.

I then tried a hair carry, but again a wave broke over us and he was gone. I dove down again and pushed him to the surface. The chin carry and hair carry had not worked, so I tried a cross-chest carry. Again I lost my hold on him as the merciless waves broke over us. He went under, and I once more dove and pushed him up to the surface. I then tried putting my M-16 sling around his chest and grabbing hold of the ends behind his head. Just as I was getting both ends together, another wave forced us apart and he again went under the waves. I surface dove again and pushed him up.

This time an undertow grabbed me and started pulling me further out to sea. I fought my way to the surface and looked around, but the man had gone under again. I surface dove two or three more times in an attempt to locate him, but I could not. The swimmer on the rock was no longer there, so I thought he had swum to shore. I was extremely exhausted by now. Trying to pull an unconscious man holding a water-filled air mattress in waves eight to ten feet high had drained me.

My next thought was to lie on my back and rest, but when I did this my arms and legs began to cramp. I knew this was not a good sign. I was so exhausted I was hallucinating, so I rolled back over and started swimming for the shore. I looked toward shore and saw my wife on the shoreline motioning for me to come out of the water. I remember thinking, "What am I doing out here when my wife is on shore?" As I was swimming towards the land, everything was turning gray. I did not realize I had gone under the water.

The next thing I knew I was clinging to a coral cliff that was about ten feet high. I called for help, but I was so full of salt water that nothing came out. The only thing to do was to pray. I remember saying, "My God, I need your help." The next wave that hit me pulled me off the face of the cliff. I yelled, "GOD, I need your help!" The next wave broke under me and lifted me up the face of the ten-foot cliff and deposited me on top. It is only by divine grace that I was able to get out of the water. Once again, God showed His love and mercy toward me.

When I reported in to the sergeant of the guard, I was told to take the rest of the night off and to return to my unit. For whatever reason, I was still holding the sling to my weapon. The sergeant had picked up my weapon from the rocks on the shore and handed it back to me. I put the sling back on it and returned to my unit.

When I got to my unit, the male nurse on duty at the A+D station (Assessment and Diagnostic) told me that the man I had put on the rock had been admitted to my ward for observation. I went to see him. As I walked onto the ward, he saw me and began to yell. He thought he was seeing a ghost.

An inquest into this event was held. Command Sergeant Major Davis initially wanted to court martial me for leaving my guard post without being properly relieved. During the inquest he asked me how I got out of the water. I told him, "The hand of God reached down and pulled me out of the sea by the seat of my pants." He was not impressed with that answer, but it was the only one I had for him.

Later I found out that a helicopter had dusted-off the man on the rock and that the door gunner was shooting sharks in the water around me. The chopper crew saw me go under and did not see me surface. I was about seventy-five meters off shore when they saw me go under and they thought I had also drowned.

I do not recall the name of the G.I. who drowned, nor can I recall the names of the others involved. When the inquest was completed, I was told that two Navy Seals and one lifeguard from the USO beach were summoned to the scene but refused to assist me as the waters were too dangerous. I was also informed that I had been put in for a medal.

During the decoration ceremony, when I received the Soldiers Medal of Valor, there was also a major receiving the Bronze Star. In the picture taken of the occasion, the major is standing to my left. Military protocol would say that I, as the enlisted man, should be standing to the major's left, and when we were first called out of formation, I did stand to the major's left. But a bird colonel walked up to the major and told him to stand down to the private. This did not make the major very happy, as can be seen on his face in the photos.

Major standing to my left

Bird Col. saluting me

HEADQUARTERS, AMERICAL DIVISION
APO San Francisco 96374

GENERAL ORDERS
NUMBER 8796

15 November 1968

AWARD OF THE SOLDIERS MEDAL

1. TC 320. The following AWARD is announced.

GRIFFITHS, GREGG E RA16978429 (SSAN   ), PRIVATE FIRST CLASS,
Headquarters and Company A, 23d Medical Battalion, APO 96374
Awarded: Soldiers Medal
Date action: 27 July 1968
Theater: Republic of Vietnam
Reason: For heroism not involving actual conflict with an armed enemy in the
Republic of Vietnam. Private First Class Griffiths distinguished
himself by valorous actions on 27 July 1968 while serving with
Company A, 23d Medical Battalion. On that date, Private Griffiths
was on bunker guard when a fellow soldier ran up to his position,
which was situated on a beach, and asked him to help his friend who
was drowning in the South China Sea. Private Griffiths immediately
left his position and ran down the rock cliff to a point where he saw
two soldiers in the turbulent water. Disregarding the danger to his
own life, he dived into the water and swam out to the two men. One
was a strong swimmer and was keeping the drowning man afloat. The
stronger swimmer was near exhaustion when Private Griffiths arrived
and was forced to swim to some nearby rocks for rest,   s
leaving Private Griffiths to bring the drowning soldier to safety.
The soldier had swallowed so much water that he kept sinking under
the surging waves. Time after time, Private Griffiths went down
into the water to push the drowning man to the surface. Finally,
he managed to slip his belt under the arms of the drowning man, but
by this time, he hardly had the energy to stay afloat. Realizing
that he couldn't bring the man in alone, he called for help from the
man he had relieved. Answering the call, the soldier swam back to
aid Private Griffiths. Together, they tried to bring the drowning
soldier to safety, but because of their complete exhaustion, the
the extremely rough waters, and the tremendous undertow, they were
unable to save the soldier. Private First Class Griffiths' personal
heroism, professional competence, and devotion to duty are in
keeping with the highest traditions of the military service and
reflect great credit upon himself, the Americal Division, and the
United States Army.
Authority: By direction of the President under the provisions of the
Act of Congress, approved 2 July 1926.

FOR THE COMMANDER:

OFFICIAL:

R S Temple Jr.
R. S. TEMPLE, JR.
1LT, AGC

JACK L. TREADWELL
Colonel, GS
Chief of Staff

Write-up for the Soldier's Medal for Valor

The Soldiers Medal is a higher medal than the Bronze Star, which the major was receiving. On the ranking of medals, the Soldiers Medal For Valor is the highest non-combat medal for valor that the army awards. This medal is awarded for risking one's life to save another's. It is awarded in peacetime for actions of heroism held to be equal to or greater than the level of the Distinguished Flying Cross, which is awarded for acts taking place in combat and involving actual conflict with an enemy.

Cam Ran Bay, Vietnam, reception station. This is where we spent our week of orientation. I never did like reception stations. Believe me, it wasn't the Ritz.

23rd Medical Battalion . This is where I spent most of my year.

Me sitting on jeep
Picture of me with attitude. I just had to write "Support mental health or else!!"
on the photo. The jeep belonged to the Americal division psychiatrist. This is my
daughter Danna's favorite picture of me in Nam.

Friend Mike Halper
My good friend in Nam, Mike Halper. We were in this village providing medical
aid, but "Charlie" (i.e., the Viet Cong) had told the village chief that if he accepted
any more aid from us, the village would be wiped out. Most of the people in this
photo were killed that night.

12

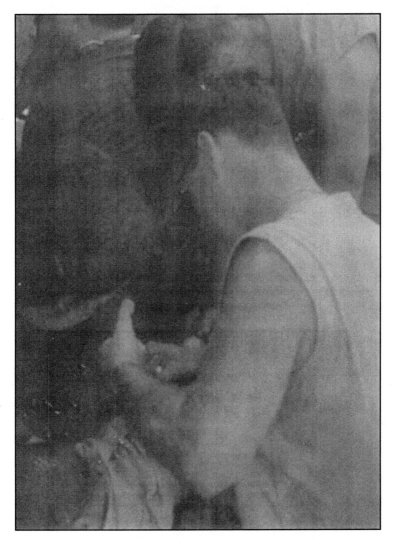

Child on my lap receiving shot
Photo of me giving a shot to a Vietnamese child.

The second medal I was awarded was the Army Commendation Medal, given for meritorious service during my tour of duty in Vietnam. Some additional stories may give you some idea why this particular medal came my way.

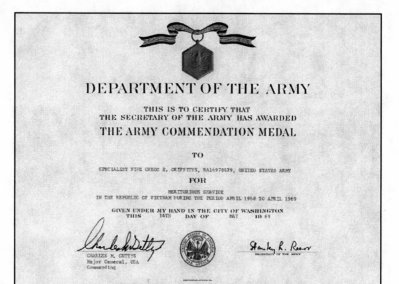

Army Commendation

Citation

BY DIRECTION OF

THE SECRETARY OF THE ARMY

The Army Commendation Medal

IS PRESENTED TO

SPECIALIST FIVE GREGG GRIFFITHS, RA16978429
UNITED STATES ARMY

who distinguished himself by exceptionally meritorious service in support of military operations against communist aggression in the Republic of Vietnam. During the period

APRIL 1968 TO APRIL 1969

he astutely surmounted extremely adverse conditions to obtain consistently superior results. Through diligence and determination he invariably accomplished every task with dispatch and efficiency. His unrelenting loyalty, initiative and perseverance brought him wide acclaim and inspired others to strive for maximum achievement. Selflessly working long and arduous hours, he has contributed significantly to the success of the allied effort. His commendable performance was in keeping with the finest traditions of the military service and reflects distinct credit upon himself and the United States Army.

Army Commendation write-up

As I have already mentioned, the division psychiatrist was stationed in our unit. I told him that when I was in college I worked and lived in a hospital psych ward. I suggested that separating the psych patients from the medical patients could be beneficial, and it would give him more time to evaluate and treat his psych patients. He suggested this to the brass at division and was given permission to go ahead with the plan. I hold the dubious honor of having established the first psychiatric holding facility in a field clearing station (not a hospital) for the Americal Division. It was a ten-bed ward, and most of the soldiers I dealt with were either suffering from drug-induced psychosis or battle fatigue. There were a number of memorable experiences, but the most dangerous involved a certain African-American soldier.

During the Vietnam era, there was some racial tension. A very large African-American soldier was in the psychiatric ward being treated for delusions. He constantly felt he had to return to his stand-down area to protect his black brothers. One evening, the night male nurse woke me and informed me this soldier was missing from my ward. He asked if I knew where he might have gone. I suggested he may have returned to his unit and that we needed to go get him as he posed a danger to others.

We went to his unit and contacted the sergeant of the guard. I informed the sergeant I thought this soldier may have made it back to his unit and that he might be armed and dangerous when we located him. I suggested the sergeant lock and load his side arm, which was a .45 caliber semi-auto pistol. He knew the man and he took my advice to lock and load. As we walked through the company area, we could hear soul music coming from one of the tents. I told the sergeant, "He's probably in that one."

I peeked through the end flap and could see him sitting on a cot at the other end of the tent. He was the only person in the tent and his back was toward us. We quietly entered, and as I approached I could see he was holding his M-16 across his lap. As I got behind him, I spoke his name and said, "It is time to return to the ward."

He stood up and swung around, leveling his M-16 at us. I blocked the weapon with my left forearm, stepped into him, used my right elbow in a sternum check blow, and disarmed him. I handed the weapon

15

backwards to the male nurse. As I was picking the soldier up off of the ground, I heard the nurse say, "Ah s*** Griff." The weapon was set on full automatic; he easily could have killed us. The situation was resolved, and he was returned to my ward. He was shipped out to Na Trang the next day for further treatment.

When I was a police officer after my military service, the community I patrolled was very wealthy. Some of the residences had their own private security guards at night. From time to time I would swing by to make sure the security personnel were okay. One night I stopped to talk with one of them and found he had been in Vietnam during the same period of time I had. We started telling funny stories, and he recounted the following tale.

He started by saying he was a Marine stationed along Highway 1. A convoy was passing a rice paddy when the lead truck was blown up. Everyone in that truck was killed. They never even called for the medic. The medic was about two-thirds of the way back in the convoy. Well, the convoy was standing still when all of a sudden there was the crack of automatic gunfire. The medic's truck, a deuce-and-a-half (a two-and-a-half ton troop or supply carrier), had come under heavy automatic gunfire. The medic bailed out of the truck and got behind the dual tires on the far side from the rice paddy. An ARVN (a South Vietnamese soldier) at his outpost began shooting back using a 50-caliber machine gun. The weapon was too heavy for the ARVN, and he could not control it. The rounds were just brushing past the medic at the rear of the truck. The poor medic didn't know which side of the truck would be safest, so he pulled out his entrenching tool and began digging a hole in the middle of Highway 1!

I asked the Marine if he was on CAP Outpost 1-1-3. He looked very astonished that I would even know the numbers. It turned out he was. When I told him I was that medic, we had a good laugh. But I can assure you, at the time that event happened, I was not laughing. I did enter the outpost later on and treated a couple of the Marines for prior wounds. The incident ended when two Cobra gun ships came in and killed the attackers in the rice paddy.

Around June of 1968, our medical unit was sent to a LZ (landing zone) out near the Tai-Cambodian border. The Ho Chi Minh Trail was near this LZ. There was an evacuation of the Ah Shau Valley in progress, and this was during one of the three Tet Offensives.

Three divisions of NVA (North Vietnamese Army) had surrounded the Ah Shau Valley. We took in a lot of wounded that week. We received them, treated and stabilized them, and then shipped them further back for more definitive care. During this time we took some sniper rounds through the ceilings of our medical tents. No one was ever hit, but they sure came close.

During some down time, Specialist-6 John Simmons and I went swimming in a small pond near the LZ. A Vietnamese boy was walking toward our clothes when Simmons asked that I get to his pants before the kid did, as there were two new containers of Morphine curettes in his pants pocket. I exited the water and went for the pants. I got there just as the boy did. He looked at me and said, "You number one, G.I." He promptly dropped two grenades at my feet. One was a fragmentation grenade and the other was for a M-79 grenade launcher. I dove into the water yelling, "GRENADE!!" Neither went off, and when I surfaced, the boy was gone. The pin in the hand grenade was still in place. Simmons and I got dressed, left the pond, and gave the grenades to an infantry unit on the LZ. The LZ was later evacuated as the three divisions of NVA bore down on our location.

I was considered a ward master even though I did not have the rank of one. One morning, just prior to 6:00 A.M., we were having our morning meeting in the A+D station. Suddenly, we heard explosions in the motor pool area. The concussions were so close that bottles in the pharmacy fell off the shelves.

I knew we were under another rocket attack, and I started running for the wards. I could see the rockets being walked through the motor pool and toward the wards. We said the rockets were "walked" through because each time the enemy launched a rocket against us, they would notice where the rocket landed and then change the range to do more damage. The rockets "walked" closer and closer to their target. At one point, I had to lean into a raised mound of dirt as a 122mm rocket landed just above me and exploded. I then jumped back up and ran into a ward to find two soldiers who could not evacuate because they had feet and lower leg wounds. I picked both of them up, putting one on each shoulder and ran with them to the bunkers. Our unit sustained fourteen hits that morning, but no one was injured.

Some time later, as I was rotating out of Nam through Da Nang, I was standing at the gate waiting to board my plane to go back to the "world" (the United States). A soldier yelled, "Hey, doc!" I looked at the G.I. and he asked if I remembered him. I told him his face was familiar, but I couldn't put a name with it. He proceeded to recount this episode to his buddies and said he had never seen anything like it. He told them that all he could see were elbows and ankles flapping in the air. We had a good laugh over it.

I was pulling the night shift on one of the medical wards. I don't remember the exact date, but I do remember it was during a dry period. At about 1:30 A.M., the sirens from CLDC (Chu Lai Directional Center) started sounding. This meant a rocket attack, causing me to evacuate my ward—except for one patient who could not move as he had intravenous tubes in him, along with leg and feet wounds. As I evacuated the ward, I assured him I would be back.

I returned and covered him with a mattress from an adjacent bed. I put my flack jacket on and stood, leaning over his head for his protection. Our unit received two or three rockets during that attack, but no one was injured. At the time of the attack, I wasn't really thinking about Scripture, but when recounting this incident some years later, John 15:13 came to mind:

The greatest love you can show is to give your life for your friends.

—(GW)

Of course I did not die in this attack, and I was not even harmed, but I guess I was willing to protect this soldier. Too many medics died trying to save those they did not know but who desperately needed help.

Orders to rotate out of Vietnam would normally arrive anywhere from forty-five to thirty days prior to the end of the tour. I was under thirty days and had not received any orders to rotate out of the country. While speaking to my wife via the M.A.R.S. (Military Amateur Radio Station) one night, I was telling her that I had received no orders yet. She claimed to have a bad connection on her end, but she told me the orders were on the way. I asked how she knew this, and she kept saying she had a bad connection.

In a letter I received from her shortly after this conversation, she informed me that she was working with a man who was a colonel in the Air Force Reserve. Apparently, she told him of my situation. He phoned the Pentagon and spoke with a lieutenant. He identified himself by rank and told him I had not yet received orders to rotate out of Nam. He told the lieutenant he wanted me to be stationed on a quiet base upon my return. The lieutenant informed the colonel that the Pentagon had no record of me even being in Vietnam. In any event, my orders were cut and a courier was dispatched from the Pentagon to Chu Lai, Vietnam.

My executive officer requested I come to his office. When I arrived he was holding my orders with a rather stern look on his face. He asked, "Griffiths, do you know the chain of command?" I asked if he wanted it from the top down or the bottom up. He said he really did not care. "But be informed that the chain of command does not go: wife, colonel, Pentagon!" I simply responded with, "Well, whatever works, sir."

Back in the States

My tour ended in April of 1969. I flew back to the States on my birthday. We crossed the International Dateline, so I got two birthdays that year. I still had eighteen months of service obligation left, so I was sent to a "quiet" army base in upstate New York.

It was nice to be back in America. Vietnam was one of those experiences I would wish on no one. At the same time, I would not trade that year for anything. I found out quickly what I was made of, and I learned a lot about the medical field. I left Vietnam with the rank of Specialist 5th Class, which is the same as a Sergeant E-5.

What most people did not know about this returning vet was that I was a doper and a very heavy boozer. Since I had my own ward in Nam, there was no accountability for the medication I kept in my own little pharmacy on the ward. At one point I was really hooked on Ritalin, but I knew I could not continue the drugs back in the States. I did manage to get off the drugs, but the alcohol played a very big part in my life over the next five years.

I tell these stories for a number of reasons. These are events that happened in my life. They also demonstrate God's care and love, along with His desire to bring me to salvation through Jesus Christ. There were a number of times other medics took my place on convoys and dust-off missions and did not return. In retrospect, if God had not had His hand on me, I may not have survived. When I did return home, a friend looked at me and stated, "You are alive. From all that I heard about what you were doing, I thought for sure you would be dead."

I had a thirty-day leave when I got back. Since I was married and was an E-5, the army would move my household goods to my next duty station. I thought it was a good idea to go to the base, set up housing, and make sure I had an address to which to ship our household goods. When my wife and I arrived at the Seneca Army Depot, we caused no end of problems.

First, I had my orders, but no one in the dispensary was aware I was being assigned there. We got that cleared up and my quarters were assigned. I was to be the dispensary specialist. That meant I was going to be doing everything from medical records to ER, lab work, X-ray, and heading up the nuclear monitoring and decontamination team.

Then, secondly, I caused a traffic jam at the exit gate. I mentioned earlier that in Vietnam, when we came under attack, the CLDC would blow a siren. At Seneca Army Depot they blew a siren at 4:00 P.M. to tell the civilian workers it was time to go home. It was 4:00 P.M. when we were leaving the base. I heard the siren sound and I saw people running. We were at the exit gate. I quickly got out of my car and crawled under it. As far as I knew, we were under attack. There were people yelling at me and horns honking, but I wasn't moving. A security person told me it was okay. I got back into my vehicle and went immediately to the dispensary, which was right by the gate. They explained the siren to me. They now knew they had a strange person reporting to their base.

After my leave, I reported for duty and checked in through the Provost Marshall's Office (PMO). The provost marshall was a very tall, well-built, African-American man. There were three or four of us Nam returnees in his office, and five others in the room who were not. Remember I said it was a quiet base? Well, not exactly. They blew off old ordinance from time to time, and this was one of those times.

20

During the lecture by the provost marshall, some ordinance was exploded and we Nam vets tipped over chairs, dove under desks, or ran out of the room. The others laughed at us—except for the provost marshall. He told those men to stop laughing. When they had experienced what we had, they could then laugh, but not until. I began having other numerous experiences that, when startled, threw me into either a fight or flight reaction.

One medic I worked with thought it would be fun to startle me. I was pulling CQ (Charge of Quarters) one night. I was walking through the dispensary turning off lights, and I did not know anyone else was in the building. He was hiding behind a door. As I passed by the door, he jumped out and grabbed me from behind. I spun and hit him numerous times and then finished him off with a side kick. As he lay on the floor in a lot of pain, I apologized but told him never to startle a Nam vet. He never did that again.

There was a New Year's Eve party at the NCO Club 1969-1970. From the time I had returned from Nam until then, which was eight months, I had no emotional release from the horrors I had witnessed in war. My wife was concerned and thought I was emotionally stoic.

I bought a $10 chit book for drinks. At the time, a shot of booze was $.25. That meant I could have nearly 40 shots. At about 4:00 P.M., my wife and I went to the NCO Club with our neighbors. I started by drinking triple shots of bourbon with coke. Later I went to singles and then doubles. We were sitting at a table with other medics back from Nam. The more we talked, the more we drank, and the more we drank, the more we talked. No one was embellishing their stories; we were just talking about a lot of what we did. My wife was becoming somewhat freaked by all of this, as I had not told her much of what I did overseas.

At about 1:30 A.M. we were ready to go home. I am sure that my blood alcohol was good to -40degrees. My neighbor was driving and the windows were a little foggy. I held my head out the window navigating and yelling, "Kill a guke for God." When we got home, the real "fun" began.

First off, as I got out of the car, I fell over sideways into a snow bank, so I was now half covered in snow. When we got into our quarters, the heat hit me and I began to feel sick. I went into the bathroom, knelt before the porcelain throne, and began vomiting. I then began crying and hyper-ventilating at the same time. I was a mess. My wife called the dispensary, and they called the doctor on duty.

The on-call doctor was my company commander. He called my wife, and when she put me on the phone I called him about every rotten name in the book. In my mind, he could not possibly understand what I was experiencing, as he had never been in combat. He sent an ambulance with the first sergeant to pick me up, and I was taken to the dispensary, given medication for the vomiting, and placed under observation all night.

When I woke up the next morning, I read my chart and found that I had alcohol poisoning. I could have died had I not received treatment when I did. I later apologized to my C.O. He told me, "Some things are best forgotten." I had my emotional release, but the nightmares, the startle reflex, and other accompanying problems continued.

The base had a chapel. My wife and I became very involved in this chapel, and I was asked to start a youth choir because I had majored in music education in college. The kids were anywhere from nine to sixteen years old. I taught them by rote, and we were singing in three-part harmony. The base commander was so excited that after our first performance he wanted to order robes for the kids and really do this up right. I asked him to please wait. They were kids, and who knew how long their interest in this choir would last? We sang about three times in four months, and then the choir died. The kids just lost interest.

However, the base commander then asked if I would teach his daughter to play the piano. I didn't feel like I could say no, so every Thursday afternoon I would go to his house to give a piano lesson. Little did I know where this would lead. At first, things went well.

Then the colonel in charge of the Q area wanted me to teach his daughter piano also. The colonel phoned me and only asked that I come to his office right away. I told my sergeant the colonel wanted to see me, but that I didn't know why. All I knew is he wanted to see me, and he wanted to see me *now*.

The Q area is a very highly secured area. It was surrounded by three fences. The center fence was electrified. As you enter this area, an outer gate opens and you drive in. Then the outer gate is closed behind you and the center gate opens. As you drive forward, the center gate is closed, and then the innermost gate opens. Bear in mind that there are MPs with automatic weapons trained on you the whole time. Once inside all those gates, we were ordered out of the ambulance, which was the vehicle I took across base to see the colonel. I had an attendant with me, and we were both staring down the barrels of automatic weapons.

The colonel had failed to tell anyone we were coming. The MPs called the colonel's aide, wanting to know why we were there. I told him all I knew was that the colonel phoned and wanted to see me in his office. While this exchange was going on my attendant, a PFC, was holding a ballpoint pen up to his eyes like a camera and started clicking it. The MPs started racking rounds in their 45s and bolts were sliding forward on the M-16s.

The business end of a .45 is not a pleasant place at which to find yourself. One of the MPs removed the pen from the attendant's hand, dismantled it, and then stomped on it. I told the PFC to knock it off. Not willing to leave it alone, he then started speaking into his wrist watch, like in a Dick Tracy cartoon. He asked, "Did you see what they did?" Needless to say, the MPs also destroyed his watch. I was escorted at gun point in to see the colonel, only to find out he wanted me to give his daughter piano lessons.

Before I left the army, my wisdom teeth were giving me a lot of trouble. We didn't have an oral surgeon on base, so I was sent into Geneva, New York, to have all four teeth removed.

Everything seemed to be going well. I was comfortable in the chair. The doctor and I had a nice conversation, my arm was strapped to a straight board, the needle was inserted, and then he put me under anesthetic. When I awoke after the extractions, I found I was strapped across my shins, my thighs, and my chest. There was an orderly literally sitting on my lap and one holding me from behind. I couldn't figure out what was happening. As best I could, I asked the doctor what happened. He asked if I was a Nam vet. I told him I'd been back only a few months. He said he had never seen anything like this. When he started up the equipment for the surgery, I came up out of the chair, started yelling orders, and tried to dive head first out of the fourth floor window. He finished his comments with, "You must have seen a lot of action over there."

I apologized as best I could.

Out of the Army

I was scheduled to leave the army in the late part of September, 1970. I had to start planning what I was going to do when I got out. My oldest daughter, Erica, was now two months old, and I needed a job to support my family. I tested with the Hennepin County Sheriff's Office in Minneapolis, Minnesota. I scored high enough to be hired as a senior deputy sheriff, and thus began my career in law enforcement.

When I interviewed for the sheriff's office, there was still much civil disobedience over the Vietnam War. The night before I was scheduled for the interview, the National Guard Armory was bombed. I was asked by one of the members of the interview panel why I wanted to become a police officer. I told him that I wanted a legal right to "carry a gun and bust heads." I was quoting a soldier who had been on my ward in Nam. One evening we were listening to a news broadcast from the States, and they were talking about the riots. Later that night I heard one of my patients crying. He had badly injured legs from a tripped booby trap and was in a lot of pain. I asked him if he needed pain medication. He said, "No, doc, I want my helmet and weapon, because I want to swim home and bust some heads." He was angry and so was I. One could not make a statement like that today and get hired. But it was the right statement for that time and place. I was hired, but I still needed to be released from the army.

The army was offering early outs for those going into law enforcement. I needed a two-week early out as I had a start date with the sheriff's office. I explained the situation to my first sergeant. He told me that even if the army gave me the early out and if my orders did arrive in the next three days, I still could not process out of the army in time to make my start date with the sheriff's office in Hennepin County.

The dispensary at which I was working was attached to Fort Devons, Massachusetts. That was nearly three hundred miles away from where I was. In our dispensary was a civilian doctor, Dr. Benjamin Eisenberg.

Eisenberg was a short, Jewish man, who seemed to know how to get things done. He was a GS-18 or 20, which put him on par with a general in the military. He phoned Fort Devons and told them I needed both the early out and the orders to rotate out of the army. Not only was the early out approved immediately, but my orders were hand carried from Fort Devons to Seneca Army Depot. They arrived within forty-eight hours of my conversation with my first sergeant, who could not believe this was happening so fast. I guess God has a way of expediting things

The next week was a whirlwind. I got my wife and daughter on a plane to fly back to Minnesota, and then I made arrangements for our household goods to be picked up and moved, while I finished processing out of the army the Friday before the Monday I was to start with the sheriff's office. I made the start date.

God had a plan and at that time, so did I. They weren't the same plan, at least not then, but God was at work making everything come together in His good timing.

CHAPTER TWO

LAW ENFORCEMENT

If we confess our sins, He is faithful and righteous to forgive us our sins and to cleanse us from all unrighteousness.

—1 John 1:9 (NASB)

WHEN I LEFT the military in 1970, I was stoic in personality. After experiencing the horrors of the war in Vietnam, I didn't believe there was anything that could hurt me. If I could survive that, I figured I could survive anything. I felt invincible. I was one of those people who went where angels feared to tread. It was not that I had a death wish, but there just wasn't much I feared. After receiving Jesus as Savior and Lord, what fear I may have had was even more diminished.

I had a meddling mother. She really had my best interests at heart, but she was concerned about my lifestyle. Because of the obvious dangers I faced, it was difficult for her to accept that I was cop. But I also drank and smoked, among other things, contributing to an unhealthy way of life. As my grandfather put it one time when I was offered a drink by my uncle, "There goes your mother's entire Sunday school upbringing."

My mother called a church that was about two blocks from my house and asked the minister to stop in and invite me to church. He did. My wife and I were setting up for a booze party that evening. I was so hospitable that I offered him a drink! Of course he refused, but this was the start of a new chapter in my life.

I was a frustrated deputy sheriff because I felt I was too young to be sitting in a dispatch center for three years. I had little to no street experience, and I felt that to be a good dispatcher, I really needed to experience the other side of the microphone. I kept bugging one of the road sergeants to bring me into the traffic division and get me out of dispatch. This sergeant was 6'9" and weighed 420 pounds. His partner was 6'11" and weighed 400 pounds. One night the sergeant went to the back wall of the dispatch room, put my gun belt on around his right thigh, and began walking around the room telling me I was too small for street experience and that I would be bounced around like a rubber ball. All the other guys were laughing.

I'm dispatching.

One afternoon I stopped at the church to speak with the minister who had visited my home. I told him of my frustration and asked him why God was not permitting me to work the street. The pastor told me that God was not going to give me what I wanted until He got what He wanted from me, which was my life. We prayed, and of course I told God what I thought He wanted to hear, but it was really not because I wanted to give my life to the Lord. I just wanted to work the street.

In June of 1973, a position became available with the Wayzata Police Department, a municipality on the north shore of Lake Minnetonka, just west of Minneapolis. I applied for the position and became a strong applicant. I told my lieutenant at the dispatch center that I had applied. He said I was a talented deputy and he did not want to lose me. But at the same time, he said he did not want to hold me back. What I did not know was that he was the son of the police chief of that department. I later learned he spoke to his father, and I was hired.

I was still a pretty brash cop, and during the interview I was asked what I would do if I got into a shoot-out. I told the interview panel that I probably wouldn't get into a shoot-out, but that I would use my military training if it happened. In Nam I had learned what was called "silent infiltration" (quick kill techniques), and would probably come in from behind the suspect and take him out. They hired me.

The Wayzata police department was small, with a total manpower of seven men: six officers and the chief. That meant that on any given shift each one of us, for the most part, worked alone. There were times when there would be an overlapping shift, but that was seldom. The city was only 3.5 square miles with a population of about 2,700, but with a daytime population that would swell to many thousands. We had three major shopping areas, about eight financial institutions, and a few posh restaurants. We had the busiest intersection in the state of Minnesota. It was my understanding when I started with this department that the city was the fourth wealthiest per capita in the United States. Working in this sort of a department meant that one learned to use one's brain and mouth more than one's brawn.

Three Domestic Disturbances

During the last two weeks of December, 1973, I had three calls of domestic disturbances. These are usually the nastiest and most dangerous types of calls to which an officer responds. All three situations had weapons involved and, of course, I was working alone on the shift.

The first call was to a residence of a couple I personally knew. He was a volunteer fireman on the local fire department, and she worked at the local Catholic Church. They were a young married couple who were having financial problems. Of course, the fact that he was a heavy drinker did not help. He was a laborer with few skills who pretty much followed the pattern of things he observed in his family growing up. Since his father would leave work for the bar before coming home, this young man was doing much the same.

I could hear the arguing when I arrived and knocked on the door. When the man opened the door, he was standing there holding a pistol at his side. He was clearly under the influence of alcohol so I knew this could go wrong very fast. I asked him why he was holding the weapon. He didn't even realize he was. There were a lot of thoughts about what to do racing through my mind at this point. Since I am not a quick-draw artist, and he already had a weapon in his hand, I held out my hand and suggested he give the weapon to me. He did. We were then able to sit down and talk. The argument they were having was over money. Police officers wear many hats. Sometimes they are counselors, other times they are ministers or priests; in this case, I was just trying to be a friend.

I suggested they separate for the night and let things cool down. Because he was under the influence, I was not about to let him drive anywhere. I suggested that since his wife worked at the church, maybe she could spend the night at the convent. I called the local priest and asked if that would be okay. He felt it was a good solution for the moment, and he said he would follow-up with the couple later. This was done, and that problem was resolved, at least for that night. The husband later entered treatment for alcoholism, and they were able to get their lives back on track.

The second domestic disturbance was a little more intense. There was a couple who lived across the street from city hall. I believe it was around midnight when I received a radio call to meet a lady at my police department office. She informed me her husband had just put a 30.06 rifle to her head and asked her if she was ready to die. The husband at the time was involved with another woman, and this woman was also in the residence when this event took place.

I requested back-up and got two other officers from a neighboring department to assist me. We met about a block away from the residence to discuss and plan how we were going to approach this situation. There were no S.W.A.T. teams in existence at this time in law enforcement, but we all recognized that we needed a plan before going through the front door. The officers suggested that I run through the front door and disarm the man. Jokingly, one of them said that if they heard any shooting, they would be right in. The real plan was simple: we would charge through the front door and each of us would take a room on the main floor.

We each grabbed our 12-gauge shot guns out of our squad cars and proceeded to the house. We locked and loaded. All three of us charged though the front door. About a half hour had passed since the wife first made contact with the police, so we were not sure of where the husband would be in the house. I moved immediately to the kitchen area while the other officers took the living and dining rooms. The husband was asleep in the living room with the rifle lying across his lap. His reaction time was slow, due to his alcohol consumption and sleep, so the first officer into the living-room was able to disarm him without further incident. The rifle he was holding had a round in the chamber and the safety was off.

Back then we did not have the domestic abuse laws we do today. I booked him on aggravated assault, but the wife nearly had him bailed out of jail before I could finish the booking paperwork.

The third domestic call was around 1:00 A.M. in the morning of January 1, 1974. My younger brother Bill had come out to ride with me that night. He was graduating with a double major in biology and chemistry and wanted to come on a ride-a-long to see if he wanted to pursue a career in law enforcement. He thought he might use his degree to work in a crime lab.

We had just cleared a house fire when the Orono Police Department received a domestic disturbance call. I was close, so I went to back them up. As we pulled up in front of the house, the man stuck a 16-gauge Remington, semi-automatic shot gun out of the front door and fired off a round at my squad car. As I was trying to move out of the line of gun fire, I reported to the dispatcher that a shot had been fired at me. The tires on my car were spinning on the snow-packed street, so I wasn't getting a lot of traction.

I should explain about my brother Bill. He went to college on a four-year scholarship to play football. Bill was the starting guard for Concordia College in Moorhead, Minnesota. He stood about 6'1" and weighed about 240 pounds. Picture Bill trying to squeeze under the dashboard of the squad car when the man fired at us. I told him to get out and go behind the garage on the other side of the street. He asked where I was going, and I told him I had to go in the house after the man.

That night it was about –14 degrees with a 15mph wind. That put the wind chill at about –30 degrees. The Orono cars arrived, and I was elected to take the back of the house. I could see the man and woman in a bedroom. He was holding the shot gun on her and yelling, "I'm going to kill you! I'm going to kill you!" She was screaming, "Don't shoot! Don't shoot!" This went on for quite some time. I had his chest sighted in with the .44 magnum pistol I was carrying that night, but I was concerned that if I shot him, it would discharge the shotgun into her. My other thought was that I was still in my probationary period with the department, and I did not want to lose my job because of a shooting.

I had been out in the cold weather for so long that I could no longer feel my weapon in my hand. The pistol was cocked, and I had put it on single action so that if he shot her I could just pull the trigger and, with little effort, shoot him. After the situation was resolved, I was walking around with my weapon pointed up in the air. A sergeant from another department had to carefully remove the gun when I explained that I could not feel it in my hand and that I needed help removing it. What I learned later was that the round the man shot at me when I arrived was the last round in his weapon. An Orono officer was able to get into the house and disarm him.

After disarming the man, we gathered in the kitchen of the house. The man thought that his significant other had stolen from him. He said he kept his money in a freezer located in the basement. I went to the upright freezer and pulled out foil-wrapped packets of money, bonds, and other assorted valuables. I brought some of it up to the kitchen, placed it in front of him, and asked, "Is this what you call keeping cold cash on hand?" We sent him off to jail, charging him with aggravated assault.

My brother decided against looking into a career in law enforcement after that night. As for me, if life wasn't exciting enough at this point, it was going to get even more exciting.

Chase Story

I was involved in my first high-speed chase in January of 1974. The marked squad car that I normally drove was down for service, so I was driving an unmarked car. On that day I had to go to the sheriff's dispatch center in the afternoon. On the return trip to my patrol area, I received a radio call of a shoplifting that had just occurred in the central area of the city. As I approached the city limits, I saw the suspect vehicle heading in the opposite direction. I made a U-turn and caught up to it.

It was late afternoon, and we were heading in the direction towards Minneapolis. The equipment on my car included a teardrop red light (a revolving red light that sits on the dashboard inside the windshield), wig-wag headlights (headlights that flash alternately on the left side then the right side), and my siren. When I turned all of this on, the suspect vehicle took off at a high rate of speed.

I radioed that I was pursuing the suspect vehicle. We were traveling east-bound on Highway 12, doing about 75mph. It was about 4:30 P.M., and traffic was beginning to get heavy. About ten miles east of us, other agencies were setting up a road block. As we came into the area of the road block, the suspect vehicle jumped the median, traveled between two oak trees, and proceeded east on the service road. I followed suit, but as my car went airborne, I headed straight for an oak tree. At 75-80mph I just knew this was a bad idea. I leaned over on the front seat to avoid the steering wheel. As I landed, the car straightened out, and I was still behind the suspects.

One of the officers at the road block ran on to the service road in an attempt to stop the vehicle. The vehicle nearly ran him down. I saw him draw his weapon, and at the speeds we were traveling, I was sure to get a bullet through my rear window. But the officer did not fire. The road ahead took a sharp turn to the right, so I decided the chase had to end before someone got hurt. As the suspect vehicle began to turn, the driver applied the brakes. This raised the rear-end of their vehicle. I sped up. As the nose of the other car dropped, I applied my brakes, dropping my front end under their rear end—and then I accelerated. They lost control and I pushed them into a snow bank.

The chase was over. One of the officers at the scene told me later he wished he had had a video camera to film the take-out move I put on the suspect vehicle. He said he doubted even Hollywood could come up with a move like that. The maneuver itself is very similar to the PIT maneuver that police departments use today.

The suspects I apprehended turned out to be one couple out of about seven who had been shoplifting at numerous stores around the metro area. There were seven couples, each stealing about one thousand dollars a day of clothing and other miscellaneous items, and using one person to fence the items. Another police department in the metro area had been working this case for about three months without being able to get a handle on it. This incident brought two women suspects to justice, and the other PD was able to get enough information to close down the rest of the operation. The two ladies were found guilty in court. The driver told me after court that if she had not had her passenger with her, the chase could have been more fun.

Now, where did God come into play in this incident? Remember the oak tree I was going to wrap the squad car around, the big one in the median? As Minnesota can be very snowy in January, I asked the deputy from the sheriff's crime lab to photograph my tracks in the snow. He looked at them and refused. He said no one would believe the pictures. Have you ever seen the cartoon picture of the skier heading for a tree when the ski tracks go on either side of the tree? This was not quite that dramatic, but the left side tire tracks do head into the tree and land on the other side. I don't know what exactly happened, but there was no tree damage to the squad car and no damage to the tree.

Even though I did not put God totally in control of my life, He was without question in control of all the circumstances surrounding my life. I believe beyond all doubt that God spared me, protected me, and rescued me, when I didn't even know I needed it.

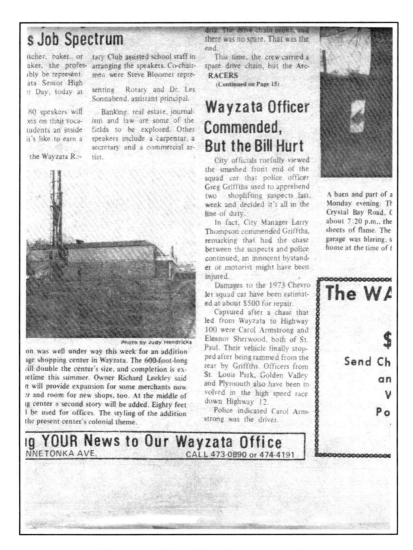

Newspaper write up about damage to squad car

CHAPTER THREE

CONVERSION EXPERIENCE AND THE BESTOWMENT OF GIFTS

For the gifts and the calling of God are irrevocable.

—Rom. 11:29 (NASB)

ONE OF MY cousins came to visit in late July of 1974. He was involved in a street ministry in Tucson, Arizona, and I believe he was still in the Air Force at that time and had been transferred from Arizona to a base in North Dakota. During his stay with us, my cousin began speaking of things spiritual. He was raised, as I was, in a very conservative church. He commented to me one day that we had been raised much the same, and he could not understand why I smoked. I told him that I not only smoked, but I also drank, and that if he tried to take the bottle away from me, he would probably hear words that would make a sailor blush. That didn't seem to startle him.

Over the next few days my cousin kept talking to me about the Lord and the spiritual gifts He has to give. He was talking about the baptism and the in-filling of the Holy Spirit. Now, I am not going to take a strong theological or doctrinal stand one way or the other on this controversial issue. There are those who believe this baptism occurs at the time of conversion, while others believe it is a separate working of the Holy Spirit after conversion. All I know is what happened to me.

On the evening of August 7, 1974, my cousin asked me if I wanted to receive the Spirit's gifts and the power that goes with the gifts. Much like Simon the magician, as recorded in Acts 8:18-24, I felt that if I had the gifts of knowledge and wisdom, I could be the greatest cop that ever patrolled the streets in my city. With those gifts, I could have foreknowledge of crimes before they happened, and then I would be able to make arrests as they happened. Or, if some criminal activity occurred when I was off-duty, I could quickly solve it because the Lord would tell me who committed the crime. I was out for my own glory, not God's. Satan said about the same thing, as recorded by the prophet Isaiah:

> But you said in your heart, "I will ascend to heaven; I will raise my throne above the stars of God, And I will sit on the mount of assembly In the recesses of the north. I will ascend above the heights of the clouds; I will make myself like the Most High."
>
> —Isaiah 14:13-14 (NASB)

It was about 10:30 P.M. when we started praying. We prayed for over an hour, but nothing was happening. My thought was that this was getting me nowhere. My cousin asked if anything was happening. When I said no, he told me to keep on praying. I really believed at this point that praying to receive the baptism of the Holy Spirit was a real waste of time. I knew of things spiritual, but in my mind this sort of thing was too far out. I was finding it very difficult to believe that any part of the Trinity was going to pay me a visit, much less empower me to do the works that Jesus did, or have the authority to freely give to anyone who believes.

Shortly after midnight a voice spoke to me. I love the apostle Paul's expression from his second letter to the Corinthians:

> I know a man in Christ who fourteen years ago— whether in the body I do not know, or out of the body I do not know, God knows— such a man was caught up to the third heaven.
>
> —2 Corinthians 12:2 (NASB)

Like that man, I was "caught up" and I heard these words: "Gregg, how can I give you these gifts when you are not even mine?" Someone just called me by name, and it sure wasn't my cousin. There were only two people in the room, and my cousin was not speaking to me at this point. Then I recognized that voice. It was God! I faced the startling realization that I was not a member of God's family.

"Lord," I pleaded, "we have had this sort of conversation before, but I never really felt You were present. I really do want to get serious about You, but I need to know You are right here, right now, listening to what I am saying."

August in Minneapolis is hot and humid, and we did not have air conditioning in the house. It was after midnight and there was no breeze outside. Houses in south Minneapolis are rather close together. As I recall, there was no traffic moving outside. Our house was less than a mile from the Minneapolis/St. Paul International Airport, yet there were no planes landing or taking off. In the house, my daughter was asleep and my wife was in the bedroom.

I was sitting on the floor of my living room, sweating and wearing a T-shirt and cutoffs. Suddenly, the curtains on the north end of the living room began to move, and there was a light breeze that moved along the floor. This wind rested on my lap. I put my moist right hand out to my side (or to the south of the wind), but the breeze was not hitting my hand. This wind rested only on my lap. The only thing I could say, in a quiet respectful voice was, "Hi, Lord."

God was paying me a personal visit. I cannot begin explaining how wonderful and, at the same time, how unsettling this can be. I knew the plan of salvation. I had actually been through the Navigators program, and I knew the Four Spiritual Laws. On occasion, I had even witnessed to others. I had some head knowledge about God, but I had never had any heart knowledge.

I knew I had to repent of my sin, ask Jesus Christ to come into my life, allow Him to clean up and take control of my life, and begin living for Him rather than for me. This was a very moving and unsettling moment because I believed for years I was already a part of God's family. In actuality, I knew I was not living like a family member, but I thought I was safe.

This was very strange. I had said to God that I needed to know He was right here, right now, listening to me, and that He was manifesting Himself to me just as I had asked. With God's personal visit to me, how could I not accept a gift from Him? I then spoke in tongues for the first time. I received first the gift of salvation, and then the gift of the Holy Spirit. The Creator of all things was in my house.

I then asked the Lord to cleanse my house. My life had been cleansed, and now my house needed cleansing. There had been many drunken parties held there, along with indecent, disgusting, and obscene events. What I witnessed next was extraordinary. The walls began making a banging or vibrating noise, as if a huge truck passed by outside that was large enough to shake the foundations. The windows rattled. There was a wind going all throughout the house from the living room and traveling to the basement and the second floor of the house.

At this point I was facedown on the living room floor before the Lord. It was as though a pressure held me down on the floor and told me not to look around or get up. There was something very awesome occurring. In reflection, I realize I was on holy ground. The Lord really was present and it was wonderful. I don't believe my cousin had ever witnessed anything like this before, and he, too, was flat on his face as the Lord moved mightily through my house.

I went to bed that night feeling a lot of peace in my life for the first time. I was determined not to say anything to my wife about what had just happened because I wanted to see how real all of this was. I knew what had happened to me, but being the skeptical cop I was, I needed more verification.

The next morning my wife woke me up. She had gone from the bedroom to the living room, did an about face, and came back into the bedroom. She woke me and then asked me what had happened in the house during the night. I asked what she meant. She stated that the house not only smelled clean but felt clean. I related my experience to her. What I didn't know was that at the time I was praying in the living room, she was also praying in the bedroom.

We sat on the couch discussing what had occurred. Suddenly, we both got up at the same time, went into the kitchen, opened the cabinet containing all of our liquor, and started dumping booze down the sink. We dumped over $70 worth, and in 1974 that was a lot of booze. The parties were over.

When I spoke in tongues earlier, I thought what I had spoken was Latin. I had never studied Latin in school, so there was no way for me to understand the language. I sang music in both high school and college that was in Latin, but I never took a course in it.

I went to a good friend, a Frenchman who had attended a Catholic seminary in France. I believed he might know Latin, and I knew that he and his wife had experienced the baptism in the Holy Spirit some years earlier. I told him of my experience and related what I had spoken. He looked at me and told me it was not Latin. He then went to some old books he had and began digging through them. After some time, he surprised me by saying, "I believe the language you were speaking was the Roman language spoken at the time of Jesus." He went on to say that the closest he could get to interpreting what I said was, "It will be completed in the Spirit." I felt excited about this and so did he.

My conversion experience combined my baptism in the Holy Spirit and my in-filling—all in one wonderful moment. My life was changed forever.

Those who knew me before my experience with Christ saw an immediate change. A lot of the cops with whom I worked and socialized were convinced I had gone over the hill and far away. There is so much more to tell, and as I explain and give examples of each of the spiritual gifts, perhaps readers will begin to see why so many cops thought I was crazy. I formed many strange and wonderful relationships due to all of this. I thought I was pretty wonderful, and others thought I was pretty strange!

CHAPTER FOUR

A BRIEF OVERVIEW OF THE GIFTS

Truly, truly, I say to you, he who believes in Me, the works that I do shall he do also; and greater works than these shall he do; because I go to the Father. And whatever you ask in My name, that will I do, that the Father may be glorified in the Son. If you ask Me anything in My name, I will do it.

—John 14:12-14 (NASB)

Now concerning spiritual gifts, brethren, I do not want you to be unaware. You know that when you were pagans, you were led astray to the dumb idols, however you were led. Therefore I make known to you, that no one speaking by the Spirit of God says, "Jesus is accursed"; and no one can say, "Jesus is Lord," except by the Holy Spirit. Now there are varieties of gifts, but the same Spirit. And there are varieties of ministries, and the same Lord. And there are varieties of effects, but the same God who works all things in all persons. But to each one is given the manifestation of the Spirit for the common good. For to one is given the word of wisdom through the Spirit, and to another the word of knowledge according to the same Spirit; to another faith by the same Spirit, and to another gifts of healing by the one Spirit, and to another the effecting of miracles, and to another prophecy, and to another the distinguishing of spirits, to another various kinds of tongues, and to another the interpretation of tongues. But one and the same Spirit works all these things, distributing to each one individually just as He wills. For even as the body is one and yet has many members, and all the members of the body, though they are many, are one body, so also is Christ.

—1 Cor. 12:1-12 (NASB)

I N *DAKE'S ANNOTATED Reference Bible*, Finis Jennings Dake has divided the gifts that are listed in 1 Corinthians chapter twelve into three major groupings. The first grouping is gifts of revelation, which includes wisdom, knowledge, and the discerning of spirits. The second group is gifts of inspiration, including prophecy, diverse kinds of tongues, and the interpretation of tongues. The third group represents gifts of power, such as faith, healing, and miracles. The order in which the gifts are listed does not in any way reflect the greatest to the least of the gifts. This means that having the gift of wisdom is not greater than having the gift of healings. The same Spirit gives each of the gifts, and they are given to believers as the Holy Spirit deems necessary.

There are those who teach that the gift of tongues is the initial evidence of having received the baptism of the Holy Spirit. In fact, I experienced this gift first. But what if the Holy Spirit wanted to give me wisdom as the first gift to be a sign of having received the indwelling of the Spirit? I do not believe we can dictate what the Holy Spirit will and will not give us. These are gifts from God the Father, through the Holy Spirit. On our birthdays, most of us do not tell others what sort of gift we want. Even if we do, that is no guarantee we will get what we ask for. Does the clay on the potter's wheel tell the potter what it wants to become? A gift is a surprise. And really, what have we done to deserve any gifts at all from the Father? The Holy Spirit and the gifts are given because our Father in heaven said He would give them.

If you then, being evil, know how to give good gifts to your children, how much more shall your heavenly Father give the Holy Spirit to those who ask Him?

—Luke 11:13 (NASB)

When I acknowledged Jesus Christ as my Savior, Redeemer, and Lord, I told Him I wanted to serve His Kingdom. The Holy Spirit was now in residence, and the Spirit brought the gifts necessary for me to

44

serve the Lord as He wanted me to serve and glorify Him. At the same time, I wanted to see the Bible come alive in my life, in those around me, and in my everyday living. I took the stance that if it's in the Bible, it's true.

> Remember those who led you, who spoke the word of God to you; and considering the result of their conduct, imitate their faith. Jesus Christ is the same yesterday and today, yes and forever.
>
> —Heb. 13:7-8 (NASB)

If Jesus Christ is the same yesterday and today and forever, then the gifts of the Holy Spirit are for today as much as they were for the first church at the time of the apostles. When I became a Christian, I wanted to see these things happen in my own life experience, and the Lord did not fail me. He brought the Scriptures alive, and often I just stood back and watched the Master work.

Because the Spirit of the Lord dwells in all believers, we are constantly in God's presence. It is through Jesus Christ alone, His completed work on the cross, and His resurrection and ascension that we have any access to the divine throne of grace.

I want to offer some greater detail to each of the gifts. As I stated earlier, this is not a theological treatise, but rather a book centered on how God has used me in reference to the spiritual gifts. This book is not in a chronological or time sequence of events. It is organized by the gift groupings. I pray my readers will be encouraged to step out boldly in the use of the gifts God has provided. He is an awesome God!

CHAPTER FIVE

GIFTS OF REVELATION

Wisdom

ONE OF THE Greek words for wisdom is *sophia*. This is the word that the apostle Paul used for wisdom in 1 Corinthians 12:8: "For one is given the word of wisdom through the Spirit" (NASB). *Vine's Expository Dictionary of New Testament Words* draws a contrast between *sophia* and *phronesis*, two of the words for wisdom in Greek. "While *sophia* is the insight into the true nature of things, *phronesis* is the ability to discern modes of action with a view of things, results. While *sophia* is theoretical, *phronesis* is practical."

I believe the gift of wisdom is not so much hearing the question that another asks, but seeing through that question to the hidden question lying behind the initial question. It is then giving the answer that the person is really looking for. A very good example of this is found in the gospel of John, when Jesus was talking with a Pharisee named Nicodemus. On the surface, it sounds like Nicodemus is going one direction with the conversation, but Jesus saw through it and gave Nicodemus the real answer he was looking for:

> Now there was a man of the Pharisees, named Nicodemus, a ruler of the Jews; this man came to Him by night, and said to Him, "Rabbi, we know that You have come from God as a teacher; for no one can do these signs that You do unless God is with him." Jesus answered

and said to him, "Truly, truly, I say to you, unless one is born again, he cannot see the kingdom of God." Nicodemus said to Him, "How can a man be born when he is old? He cannot enter a second time into his mother's womb and be born, can he?" Jesus answered, "Truly, truly, I say to you, unless one is born of water and the Spirit, he cannot enter into the kingdom of God. That which is born of the flesh is flesh, and that which is born of the Spirit is spirit. Do not marvel that I said to you, 'You must be born again.' The wind blows where it wishes and you hear the sound of it, but do not know where it comes from and where it is going; so is everyone who is born of the Spirit."

—3:1-8 (NASB)

Orono Police Department circa 1981

By August of 1982, I had already left the Wayzata Police Department and joined the Orono Police Department. I was working a 10:00 A.M. to 6:00 P.M. shift. It was a sunny, hot, and humid day, and as I drove into the parking lot at the police station I could see my chief running from the building to his squad car. He yelled at me to jump into his car with him. As we were heading toward Wayzata, he informed me that Sgt. Anderson, who worked for the Wayzata Police Department, had been shot and the suspect was still at large. We were heading for the shooting scene.

Traffic was not heavy, and the chief was a good driver, so we were really moving fast. Many thoughts go through an officer's mind in situations like this. What does the suspect look like? Will he shoot at me also? Will I be able to return fire? Believe me, there was prayer going up to heaven in that eight-minute trip. As we raced to the area of the first shooting, we were given an update from the dispatcher that two employees at the Wayzata City Hall had just been shot. Other officers were already at the first shooting scene, so we diverted from the officer-involved shooting to render aid at Wayzata City Hall.

We arrived at city hall the same time as the paramedics. The chief and I entered first to secure the scene to make sure it was safe for them to enter. After that, I started assisting the employees who were shot. They really weren't in city hall per se, but they were workers in the municipal court section attached to Wayzata City Hall. The shooting suspect had simply walked into the reception area and shot the two employees who were sitting behind the desk. One was a lady who was shot at close range, and the other was a man who had been shot in the leg.

As all of this is going on, a fellow officer from Orono PD arrived. We were told by a witness that the shooter left the scene by running through the courtroom and out through the double glass doors at the rear of the courtroom. The chief, the other officer, and I headed out the same way. When the witness said the suspect ran through the glass doors, he was correct. Since they were locked, the suspect had literally jumped through them. There was glass all over the place.

As we left the building and began the search, we formed a triangle. I took the point, the chief was to my right and behind me, and the other officer was to my rear and off to my left side. As we searched for this person, we reached the street behind city hall. Walking west on the street, the officer behind me yelled, "Freeze!" I spun around and saw a man in the bushes. He was the man who ran *through* the glass doors, but he was not the suspect. I personally knew the suspect, and this was not him. This man was a customer who had been at the counter when the two employees were shot. His intention was to leave the building as quickly as he could without getting shot himself. And glass doors were not going to stop him. I felt sorry for him because he had just witnessed a shooting, escaped without getting shot, and now three cops with very heavy artillery were pointing at him.

We returned to city hall and found that the two victims had been loaded into the ambulance, but the ambulance had been blocked in by other emergency vehicles. I directed the driver to drive over the grass and over a freshly planted tree. The victims survived their wounds.

The suspect had walked from city hall to the post office and decided to take his stand there. He held no hostages, but ordered everyone out of the building. There were now fifty to seventy-five police officers surrounding the post office. Eventually three S.W.A.T. (Special Weapons and Tactics) teams responded to the scene. Not only that, because we were at a post office, we had a team of federal officers. Our local team was not requested, probably because we were too close to the officer who was shot. But we were there in any event.

I took up a position on the north side of the building, along with a sheriff's deputy with whom I had previously worked. I knew the suspect so I could identify him if he exited a back door. My position covered the north and west sides of the building. A postal worker who didn't know anything about what was happening came out of the back door of the post office and was met by a lot of weapons pointed at him. I yelled to the man to come to me and told other officers that he was a postal worker and not the suspect.

The deputy asked if I wanted to go in and get the suspect. I said, "Being that I know him and the inside of the building, we should go for it." Just as we started to move, the announcement was made over the police radio that the command post had been established and all officers were to hold their positions. We went back to our original position. The perimeter of the building was secure, so we were ordered to start clearing the apartment building to the north of the post office.

I later asked my chief what his response would have been if we had entered the building to take down the suspect. He asked if it would have been before or after the announcement of the command post. I told him it would have been after the announcement. His response was humorous. He said, "I would have suspended you for three days for disobeying an order, but upon your return to duty I would have given you a commendation for your actions to end the ordeal."

And what an ordeal it was. This incident started shortly before 10:00 A.M. and now, somewhere around 4:30 P.M., a K-9 was sent into the building. The dog did a search and returned to its handler. S.W.A.T. officers entered the building and found that the suspect had shot and killed himself. Ironically, he used Sgt. Anderson's weapon in the suicide.

The final tally of the shootings was two dead: Sgt. Anderson and the suspect. In addition, the shooter wounded three other people—the two people at the court and a Minnetonka police officer in front of the post office.

Where does wisdom come into this story? When the chief and I got back to the PD, we talked. He stood in his office looking out his window and said, "Really makes you think."

Most people might have responded with, "Yeah." But I asked, "About what?"

The chief pondered, "Did God's hand slip when Sgt. Anderson died?"

I explained to the chief that, according to the Bible, we police officers are considered to be the ambassadors of God.

> For he is the minister of God to thee for good. But if thou do that which is evil, be afraid; for he beareth not the sword in vain: for he is the minister of God, a revenger to execute wrath upon him that doeth evil.
>
> —Rom. 13:4 (KJV)

Just as any ambassador would hope his country would come to his aid if he encountered a serious problem, so we as peace officers hope that heaven would come to our aid. I then said, "Chief, the question is not whether God's hand slipped. The question is whether you are ready to meet God!" He just answered with a huff and didn't want to take the discussion any further.

I find it interesting that when a spiritual subject is broached, and the answer to the question is not really what someone *wants* to hear but what they *need* to hear, the subject is so often closed.

Knowledge

The gift of knowledge is a supernatural revelation of divine facts disclosing the plan in God's mind. It is given to persons concerning their own lives. The gift can also reveal God's plan for others, of which the person receiving the gift would have had no prior knowledge.

Before I gave my life to Christ, I wanted this knowledge or insight for my own glory. After all, what couldn't someone do with knowledge of the divine plan? When I surrendered this desire for the purpose of self-gain, the true gift of knowledge was put into practice in my life. Simon the sorcerer had a similar response in the book of Acts:

> Now there was a certain man named Simon, who formerly was practicing magic in the city, and astonishing the people of Samaria, claiming to be someone great; and they all, from smallest to greatest, were giving attention to him, saying, "This man is what is called the Great Power of God." And they were giving him attention because he had for a long time astonished them with his magic arts. But when they believed Philip preaching the good news about the kingdom of God and the name of Jesus Christ, they were being baptized, men and women alike. And even Simon himself believed; and after being baptized, he continued on with Philip; and as he observed signs and great miracles taking place, he was constantly amazed. Now when the apostles in Jerusalem heard that Samaria had received the word of God, they sent them Peter and John, who came down and prayed for them, that they might receive the Holy Spirit. For He had not yet fallen upon any of them; they had simply been baptized in the name of the Lord Jesus. Then they began laying their hands on them, and they were receiving the Holy Spirit. Now when Simon saw that the Spirit was bestowed through the laying on of the apostles' hands, he offered them money, saying, "Give this authority to me as well, so that everyone on whom I lay my hands may receive the Holy Spirit." But Peter said to him, "May your silver perish with you, because you thought you could obtain the gift of God with money! "You have no

part or portion in this matter, for your heart is not right before God. "Therefore repent of this wickedness of yours, and pray the Lord that if possible, the intention of your heart may be forgiven you. "For I see that you are in the gall of bitterness and in the bondage of iniquity." But Simon answered and said, "Pray to the Lord for me yourselves, so that nothing of what you have said may come upon me."

—Acts 8:9-24 (NASB)

The gifts of knowledge and wisdom are often paired. Knowledge is having the insight about a given situation, while wisdom, in this case *phronesis*, provides the best way to manage the situation in a practical fashion.

RAPE CASE

At first I wanted to have the gift of knowledge so I would be a better cop, to know who committed what crimes, and to be able to solve cases. The Lord worked through me in the following case. Early in 1983, in the last department I worked in, there was a teenage girl who was raped in her own home, at night, in her bedroom on New Year's Eve. When the investigating officer from our department was unable to get a handle on the suspect, the case was turned over to the Sheriff's Criminal Division. They interviewed people, did some follow-up with the crime lab, but were unable to solve the case.

There was a young officer I worked with who had an attitude. He was fun for the most part, but he was very cynical for someone so young. I stayed late one evening at the PD, going over some of my cases, when this young officer approached me. We started talking about the rape case and he asked me, "Why don't you ask God who did it?" I told him I had done that already and the answer was on the way. He then asked me, "How many cases have you solved using God?" In fact, I had about an eighty-percent clearance rate by arrest on my investigations, and a one-hundred-percent conviction rate in court.

God answers every prayer. It may not be the answer we want, or it may not be in the timing we think is important, but He hears and answers every prayer. In the tenth chapter of Daniel, the prophet Daniel prayed for twenty-one days about a situation. The angel Gabriel told the prophet that God had heard his prayer from the first day he prayed, but Satan had prevented him from delivering God's message until another Archangel, Michael, assisted in getting the message through.

THE ANSWER

When I received the answer, it wasn't in the form of a voice one could hear. Rather, a series of events led to the answer. Back in the 1980s, we didn't have DNA testing. I began putting some situations together, and finally one night I was able to confront the rape suspect and his mother. The suspect was a juvenile, so I needed to go through the parents to interview him. I informed the mother and the suspect that I wanted them in my office the next day at 5:00 P.M.

Shortly before they were due in my office, the family attorney phoned and stated that the young man would not be able to come to my office as he had been admitted to a psychiatric ward in one of Minneapolis' largest hospitals. The attorney said that the young man apologized for his actions even though I had not told the mother or the suspect why I wanted to see them in my office. I asked the attorney for what actions was the young man apologizing. At this point the attorney realized what he had said and would not give me any further information.

The sheriff's crime lab had collected seminal fluid from the crime scene that contained type B blood. The victim herself was blood type A. I called the captain of the Hennepin County Sheriff's Criminal Division and asked if I could get the case back. He was not opposed to do it, as they had hit a dead end, but he allowed me to take a look. I reviewed everything that had been collected, including the case reports and interview tape recordings. I then wrote the affidavit for the court, requesting a search warrant.

I showed the affidavit to my chief, who looked at me quizzically and told me that I was "dangerous," a comment I will explain later in the story. What I wanted to do was collect a blood sample so we could determine what my suspect's blood type was. Then I wanted him to chew on gauze so we could determine if he was a secretor of blood in his bodily fluids.

Since I felt it was always a good thing to take a search warrant for sexual crimes to a female judge, I took the affidavit to one. She read over the affidavit, signed it, and said to go get him. I also told a chemist friend what I was doing. She worked at the Minnesota State Crime Bureau and said she would be standing by to receive the evidence for immediate processing.

With the search warrant in hand, I went to the hospital. It was the first time this particular hospital had ever had a search warrant served for a person's bodily fluids. I stopped at the hospital's security office first to get a guide to the hospital's psychiatric ward. I contacted the head nurse, showed her the warrant, and explained what I needed her to do. She refused to do anything until the head psychiatrist, hospital administrator, and their attorneys could be notified.

The doctor said he would not permit this intrusion. The head administrator phoned the hospital's attorneys and was advised not to permit this. And so it went. I phoned one of the assistant county attorneys and explained that I had a search warrant signed by a judge and that I was not getting any cooperation from the hospital. The assistant county attorney then spoke with the head administrator and told him that if they continued to refuse assistance in the execution of the search warrant, he would direct me to come to his office where warrants for "obstruction of justice" would be filed, after which the hospital employees involved would be placed under arrest.

Before long the doctor drew the blood, and the nurse had the young man chew on gauze. I now had the evidence I needed. I left the hospital and went directly to the Minnesota State Bureau of Criminal Apprehension in St. Paul, where my chemist friend was there to receive and process the evidence.

The analysis showed that the rape suspect indeed was a blood type B secretor. Statistically, only two percent of the male population having blood type B are secretors of blood into their bodily fluids. I put all the paperwork together and gave it to the county attorney. Ultimately, the young man pled guilty and the case was closed.

When this case began, no one was able to get a handle on who committed this crime. On the eve of St. Patrick's Day, there was an attempted burglary of a home about a mile and a half from the original rape scene. On the eve of Memorial Day, there was a reported Peeping Tom at the same residence. Then, on the eve of July 4, there was another report of a Peeping Tom at the same residence. I called for a K-9 unit, and the dog was able to track the suspect to his residence.

The girl who had been raped and the girl whose family reported the attempted burglary and the Peeping Toms were close friends. They also attended the same private school, so they rode on the same school bus. Coincidentally, the suspect also attended the same private school and rode the same bus.

Earlier I stated that my chief called me dangerous. His belief stemmed from other cases I had worked where I had used, in his opinion, unconventional reasoning to resolve those cases. Up to this point, the evidence in this case was circumstantial. But with the spiritual gift of knowledge I was able to put together what appeared to be unrelated information. The gift of wisdom came into play on how to collect the evidence. There are a number of ways bodily fluids can be collected, ranging from the suspect providing a sample of seminal fluid, which is what the judge wanted initially, to chewing on gauze. I felt the gauze would be the least intrusive, given the circumstances.

We have a tremendous promise found in the book of James. It is a promise with conditions, and yet the conditions are also a gift from God. It is the gift of faith for those who seek wisdom:

> But if any of you lacks wisdom, let him ask of God, who gives to all men generously and without reproach, and it will be given to him. But let him ask in faith without any doubting, for the one who doubts is like the surf of the sea driven and tossed by the wind. For let not that man expect that he will receive anything from the Lord, being a double-minded man, unstable in all his ways.
>
> —James 1:5-8 (NASB)

The secret here is to believe. In the ninth chapter of the gospel of Mark, the disciples brought a child and father to Jesus. The disciples were unable to deliver the child of demonic possession. Jesus talked with the father about the boy's situation. At the end of the story, the Lord asks the father if he believed that He, Jesus, could free the boy of this demon possession. The father's response was forthright and frank:

And Jesus said to him, 'If thou art able to believe! all things are possible to the one that is believing;' and immediately the father of the child, having cried out, with tears said, 'I believe, sir; be helping mine unbelief'.

—9:23-24 (YLT)

The boy was freed. The father confessed his belief, but he still needed help believing further. That would certainly be true for most of us. The Lord knows the hearts of men and women. *Dake's Annotated Bible* speaks to the matter of belief versus unbelief. There are two "ifs" in Mark 9:23-34. One is by the child's father, and the other one is by Jesus. Deity can use "if" just as much as humanity. In fact, God has the only lawful right to use such a term, for it is a settled fact that all things are possible with Him. So if people can quit their eternal questionings and satanic unbelief concerning God's will and power, then "all things" will be possible for the believer (Mark 9:23; 11:22-24; Matthew 17:20; 21:22; John 14:12-14; 15:7-16; 16:23-24). It is not a question of what God can do, but rather what man can do in believing God and His Word. Any question of God's will concerning anything He has already promised and provided is an excuse of unbelief and must be repented of (Mark 9:24; Hebrews 11:6; James 1:5-8). The answer to any question one has towards faith is simple belief.

INTERNATIONAL COCAINE SMUGGLER

It was not uncommon to have such a busy shift that calls began piling up. On one such day, I had stopped a man for speeding. While I was running the normal driver's license and warrant checks, dispatch responded that the man had a warrant for his arrest. I took him into custody. Just as this was happening, I received a radio call for a personal injury accident. I asked the dispatcher to start an ambulance and reported I would be responding with one man in custody. I was only a mile and a half away.

I found no one injured when I arrived at the accident sight. I started to cancel the ambulance but then I saw that the man in custody was showing symptoms of having a heart attack. I informed dispatch of the new problem developing, and when the ambulance arrived, he was transported to the hospital. After the people involved in the accident exchanged their information for the accident report, they went on their way. All of this became the backdrop for a fourth situation taking place at the same time as the accident, the arrest, and the coronary.

Our squad cars were equipped with a device known as a teleprinter. The dispatcher could send out nonverbal messages which were printed out on a piece of paper from the teleprinter. Only important messages were sent out in this fashion.

A message appeared on my teleprinter from a town in northern Minnesota which was over one hundred miles from the Twin Cities. The message concerned a stolen diamond ring worth over five thousand dollars. It included a description of the man and his vehicle. After I read the message I discarded it. After all, what were the possibilities this person would come to our city?

Two days later I was dispatched to one of the shopping centers in the city where a short-change artist was operating. A short-change artist is a person who will start to pay for an item with a large bill and then, when given the change, confuses the clerk by handing her more money from the change he receives. Usually, if the clerk is not attuned to this scam, the clerk will give back more money than was received. I had a description of the scammer, and it was verbatim to the one on my teleprinter from two days earlier. Since the original message had contained a vehicle description, I asked the dispatcher to find that message and send it out again. It took some time, but they found it and sent it out again to my teleprinter. I went to the shop where the suspect had been working, but by then he was gone.

I asked the Lord to show me the suspect's location. I felt directed to leave the first shopping center and to head for another. As I pulled into the parking lot, I saw a man leave one of the stores and walk toward his vehicle. It was a beautiful sight, for this man and his car both fully matched the communication from dispatch.

I pulled up to the man, got out of my squad car, and asked him for identification. As we were talking, a store owner approached and informed me that one of his cashiers had just been victimized by a short-change scam, and that this was the man who had done it. I placed him under arrest. I asked the man if I could look in the trunk of his vehicle and he gave me permission. There in the trunk I found the stolen diamond ring, still in the store's jewelry box. I also placed the suspect under arrest for possession of stolen property. The Lord answered my prayer to help me find this thief.

There were two county detectives working in the area, assisting the PD with the investigation. They took the suspect to jail for me. The man was arraigned and subsequently made bail. A day or so later, one of the detectives was at the county jail and was informed by a prisoner that the suspect they had booked was an international cocaine smuggler and was wanted by Interpol. At that time, the United States did not have access to Interpol files at the local level. One of the detectives had an acquaintance in a Canadian police department, and so he was contacted. I learned the suspect was, in fact, wanted by Interpol for international cocaine smuggling, but by that time he was long gone and had probably made it back to Columbia, South America.

When the defendant's court date arrived in northern Minnesota, the defendant did not. I received a phone call from one of the county sheriff's captains. I was informed the suspect had jumped bail and was asked if I knew where he might be headed. I told him possibly back to Columbia, South America, although he did have a sister who lived in Chicago, Illinois. I told the captain that at least the property was recovered. The suspect's last name was Campo, of the Campo drug cartel.

6710 CHASE! MIKE O'LOUGHLIN'S NOTES

A good friend and brother in the Lord shares another story about the gift of knowledge. The department had a pretty loose ride-along program, and Mike would ride with me on the night shift with some frequency. I felt it never hurt to have another set of eyes, and Mike was good at following my direction. He also had about five inches on me and many more pounds. When I told him to relate the story, this is what he said:

Gregg, here is how I remember things:
In the summer of 1976 we left a Sunday evening service at Jesus People Church. As we crossed Nicollet Avenue, you turned and very seriously said, "Mike, I think that this service and other things are

preparing me literally to put a gun in someone's mouth and maybe have to kill them."

I wasn't startled by this. After all, I had seen and heard many odd things with you. But after a few short seconds, I knew what you said was true. I said to you, "I believe it, Gregg, and what's more, I am going to be with you because it's coming soon." Somehow I also knew this would involve a 6700 (Plymouth Police Department) car and Highway 101. I knew I was to be ready, but of course I had no idea what I was to be ready for. My information did not seem as specific as yours.

The next couple weeks were routine. I rode along in your squad car a couple times, and I recall that the details kept coming. We did not know the nature of the call that was to come, but you knew it would be serious to the point of taking a life if need be. Conversations between us centered on this, and the Holy Spirit revealed many more details that all turned out exactly as given.

A couple weeks after the Nicollet Avenue conversation, I was riding with you late one night—a late Sunday night, or possibly an early Monday morning. We were sitting at a gas station at Wayzata Blvd. and Central Avenue, monitoring traffic, when the Hennepin County radio came alive with a loud and urgent voice: "6710 chase!" We looked at each other and almost uniformly cried out, "This is it!" We both knew this was what the preparation and prayer that had gone on for a couple weeks was for. You started up the squad car, notified dispatch you were moving into position to assist, and began heading North on 101 towards Plymouth at a high rate of speed.

After a few seconds, the Plymouth car continued with information that the Plymouth Police Department was chasing a Mercedes at about one hundred mph southbound on highway 101. We were coming fast northbound when we saw lights ahead, and from the description of the chase, we knew the car approaching us must be the vehicle in question. We also saw that 6710 was losing the race.

We blocked the road, driving towards the Mercedes with flashing lights, spotlights, and wig-wag headlights on. The Mercedes hit the ditch and stopped. You shouted into the radio that we had them stopped and gave the location. 6710 pulled up and began a foot pursuit of one of the occupants who had fled towards some woods.

You opened your briefcase and handed me the .45 caliber semi-automatic pistol you used as a backup. This was the gun you went to in times of trouble. You didn't like to be outgunned, being forced to carry a department issued .38 caliber "pea shooter." In this case, you gave the .45 to me.

You approached the vehicle which still had three or four occupants. As you covered the driver in the front, I used the .45 to lay over the hood and hold the weapon on the persons in the back seat. The dispatcher had been unable to understand your transmission as to location and was getting worried. They began calling for 6710 or 7200 (that was us), to answer. You were busy holding the gun in or by the driver's head, and the Plymouth cop was chasing the front seat passenger through the woods. So I picked up the microphone and told them that I was riding with 7200 and described the scene.

A nearby Orono Officer recognized my voice and knew the location to be correct. Other officers arrived in a short time and the event was over.

The preparation, due to the words of knowledge, kept everything under control during the situation, and it probably saved the lives of one or more of the people in the Mercedes that night.

Discerning of Spirits

I know we are not to operate our lives by experience, but rather by the Word of God. Nevertheless, it has been my experience that when it comes to discerning of spirits, many Christians automatically assume that this has to do with demonic spirits only. C. Peter Wagner states that "the gift of discerning of spirits is the special ability God gives to some members of the Body of Christ which enables them to know with assurance whether certain behavior purported to be of God is in reality divine, human, or satanic"[1] Many fellow officers really thought I was strange during my years in law enforcement. I am not one of those Christians who sees demons behind every bush, but I am readily able to discern evil when it presents itself.

Now we have received, not the spirit of the world, but the Spirit who is from God, that we might know the things freely given to us by God, which things we also speak, not in words taught by human wisdom, but in those taught by the Spirit, combining spiritual thoughts with spiritual words. But a natural man does not accept the things of the Spirit of God; for they are foolishness to him, and he cannot understand them, because they are spiritually appraised. But he who is spiritual appraises all things, yet he himself is appraised by no man.

—1 Corinthians 2:12-15 (NASB)

A detective who really epitomizes the above verses once told me that I scared him. He believed I might even view him as a demon and shoot him. This man had no spiritual understanding. A physical weapon is not effective against an entity that is spiritual. Another detective told me that he understood what I was talking about, but that I shouldn't be using spiritual gifts on duty. As if true spiritual gifts can be turned on and off. Besides, I can't think of a better place to use the gifts than on the job.

Some months later, both of these detectives met me for coffee and wanted to know what I knew about grave desecration. Even though it could be considered a word of knowledge, I did, basically, lay out their case for them, describing the age, sex, and conditions of the grave that was desecrated even though I knew nothing about their investigation. I was even able to give them a lead as to who actually committed the crime. I ended the discussion by stating, "What's the problem? Is this cop not so crazy after all?" They smiled and left, thanking me for the information.

A WITCH

One day as I was preparing to go out on patrol, a young lady I knew to be a witch from previous conversations approached my squad car. She really lit into me about how I was not allowed to stop her from worshipping the way she wished. Under the Constitution of the United States she had that right. I agreed with her, but I posed a question: "Why would you want to worship Satan when you could worship Satan's Creator?" She told me that Satan gave her more power than God could give her. I told her she was wrong, and then I told her I was going to demonstrate God's power. I simply said, "I rebuke that spirit that is in you in the name of Jesus Christ!" She took off running.

Some weeks later she approached me once again and agreed that I had more power in the name of Jesus than she had in Satan. She told me she wanted to be free of the demons she knew controlled her. I arranged a deliverance session (some would call this an exorcism) for her at my church.

As we were driving there, she again said she wanted to be set free of the spirits in her, but she was really scared. I told her I understood how she felt, but that the Lord was in control of this situation, and that if she saw this through she would be free of demonic influence in her life.

As we approached the church, a voice came out of this young woman that definitely did not belong to her. The voice was a deep, guttural sound that expressed a lot of anger. The voice told me to keep driving and not to stop at the church. I was not deterred, and as we pulled up to the church, I saw a knife coming down at my neck. I said, "Praise You, Lord." The knife stopped mid-thrust. The girl's hand was bent backward at the wrist and hyper-extended. It was in a position that one could not accomplish by oneself. Clearly, God's angels had intervened. The knife dropped out of her hand and onto the floor of the back seat. The blade of the knife never touched my skin.

She broke down in tears and told me she had no control over that. I told her again that God was in control, and it was now time to tell the demons to leave. We went into the church, met with some of the ministers, and prayed over her to be freed of demonic control. Praise God, she was released.

LADY WITH THE SHORT LEG

Between 1974 and 1977, I was involved in a ministry dealing mostly with people in the satanic occult. I was present at numerous sessions where people were delivered from demonic oppression and possession. The ministry also taught weekend seminars on the occult, and many healings took place on these occasions. These seminars were offered in churches and a variety of colleges in the upper Midwest.

At one of the seminars, there was a lady in her late fifties who had injured her leg as a child. Due to this injury, that leg quit growing. She wore a very thick sole on her shoe so she could walk in a level fashion. The lady thought God was angry with her and that this was why her leg stopped developing. She even believed she was possessed by a demon. A group of us were discussing the situation, and we came to the conclusion that she didn't need deliverance, nor was God getting back at her. What she needed was divine healing to show her the extent of God's love.

> And as He passed by, He saw a man blind from birth. And His disciples asked Him, saying, "Rabbi, who sinned, this man or his parents, that he should be born blind?" Jesus answered, "It was neither that this man sinned, nor his parents; but it was in order that the works of God might be displayed in him.
>
> —John 9:1-3 (NASB)

I was holding this woman's lower leg and heel as we prayed for her. And as we prayed, her leg lengthened in my hands. There was much rejoicing as she walked out of the room, now tilted to the other side due to the thick sole on her one shoe. She did not need to be delivered of any evil spirits, but she needed to see that God really did love her and wanted His works to be manifested in her.

I continued with this ministry for some time. The problem I was beginning to notice was that my life was so wrapped up in teaching on the occult that I was forgetting to lift up the name of Jesus. Well, this shortcoming came to a sudden halt on June 21, 1977.

STRANGE NOISES IN THE BASEMENT

On a late Sunday afternoon, I was working the middle shift when I received a radio call to see a lady living on Benton Avenue. The dispatcher put the call out this way: "See the lady at (address withheld). She is reporting strange noises in her house. I tried to determine for you if the noises are animal, mechanical (then he dropped the pitch of his voice) or other." This particular dispatcher was a deputy with whom I had worked previously. We were drinking buddies, but when I received Christ and tried to witness to him, he wanted nothing more to do with me. He believed I had really gone over the hill psychologically. I acknowledged the call and proceeded to the residence.

When I arrived, I checked out the scene and approached the house. I had never been to this residence before, nor had I had any dealings with the people who lived there. I knocked on the door and the lady opened it. She immediately started to tell me about the continual noises. I interrupted her and asked, "How long have you been practicing witchcraft?" This question surprised both of us. I had never asked a person such a question during an initial meeting. Her response was that she had just given her life to Jesus Christ two weeks earlier, but her husband was still practicing the black arts as a warlock. I told her I believed that the noise was a spiritual conflict in the house which manifested itself in noisy commotion. As I stood there talking with her, I could also hear the noise.

I asked her to take me to her husband's room. She led me into the basement and opened a door leading into a blood-red-lit room. All of the accoutrements of satanic worship were hanging on the walls. The noise was emanating from this room. She asked me what could be done about the noise, and I told her that if she was willing, we could pray over the room and the entire house and evict the cause of the noise.

She said she was willing. We prayed that Jesus would free the house and its inhabitants from the consequences of occult sin. I also prayed that the Lord would protect the woman from further disruption due to the continuing spiritual conflict between her and her husband. As we prayed and agreed together in the Lord, the noises actually quit. She looked at me and asked, "Now what?" I suggested that I would like to talk with her further to encourage her in the Lord.

While we were having coffee, the dispatcher requested I phone the dispatch center to tell him the nature of the noise. I informed him it was a spiritual conflict in the house manifesting itself in noise. He became very agitated with my response and asked what I did. I informed him that the lady and I prayed over the house and after that the noises stopped.

He began yelling at me over the phone, "You can't do that on duty!" I very calmly asked him, "What is the officer's motto?" He responded with, "to protect and serve." I said, "Right, and it doesn't say to protect physically or spiritually—does it?" With that, he slammed the phone down.

The Lord gives courage. Moses was told to "be strong and courageous, do not be afraid or tremble at them, for the Lord your God is the one who goes with you. He will not fail you or forsake you" (Dueteronomy 31:6 NASB). I saw the lady about a year later. She told me her husband had since left the occult and had given his life to the Lord. I am grateful to God for giving me the courage to do what needed to be done.

At times it becomes difficult to stand for the Lord in our secular world. This applies to me as much as anybody, but I have learned that God will give us the strength and courage to stand, because we stand in His strength and not ours. All we have to do is be faithful when we face friends, family, neighbors and our employers. Moses had to face the leader of a mighty nation, and then the million-plus people who followed him out of Egypt. So be strong and courageous. God will not fail you.

> Have I not commanded you? Be strong and courageous! Do not tremble or be dismayed, for the Lord your God is with you wherever you go.
>
> —Joshua 1:9 (NASB)

The gifts of revelation are mighty and powerful. Sometimes they are used individually, and at other times they are used in conjunction with one another. No matter the format, God is supplying the result.

CHAPTER SIX

GIFTS OF INSPIRATION

Prophecy

IN HIS BOOK, *Your Spiritual Gifts Can Help Your Church Grow,* C. Peter Wagner defines the gifts of prophecy as, "the special ability that God gives to certain members of the Body of Christ to receive and communicate an immediate message of God to His people through a Divinely-anointed utterance… Those who receive the benefit of the gift of prophecy can expect comfort, guidance, warning, encouragement, admonition, judgment and edification."[2] The apostle Paul said that "one who prophesies speaks to men for edification and exhortation and consolation" (1 Corinthians 14:3 NASB). Speaking for edification means we are not to preach or teach for the purpose of condemnation, for the Scriptures say "there is therefore now no condemnation for those who are in Christ Jesus" (Romans 8:1 NASB).

The gift of prophecy is for the purpose of building up the Church, the body of Christ. To me, it is a very exacting gift. In the Old Testament, the prophets of God had to be one hundred percent accurate one hundred percent of the time. If they were not, they were killed. Today, no one is killed for false prophecy. Some even say that for the most part, only sixty percent of the prophecies that come forth may be of God, while forty percent derive from mere human thought. Being very honest, I find this practice against Scripture. I hold to the one-hundred-percent position.

The apostle Paul admonishes church leaders always to test the spirit of the prophecy that is spoken forth. I have been in church services where this gift has been in use and the ministers have shut the speaker down because the word coming forth was not or could not be substantiated by Scripture. Church leaders are there to protect the body of Christ, and they must be in tune with God's Word in order to judge the prophetic word during a church service.

Prophecy comes in two forms. The first is *foretelling*, which is the telling of future events yet to occur. The second form of prophecy is *forth-telling*. This form is speaking to current events. Ministers often "forth-tell" in their sermons, that is, they speak about what is going on in the world. I heard a minister put it this way so as not to confuse the gift of prophecy with the gift of knowledge: "A word of knowledge would be to say there is adultery happening in this congregation; whereas the gift of prophecy would say there is adultery going on in this congregation, third row, forth seat."

Burglary Suspect

I was investigating a burglary at a residence. Based on some very circumstantial evidence and some information from an informant, I knew who committed the crime. I called the suspect in for questioning. During the interview, he repeatedly denied any involvement in this burglary. He stated he would even take a polygraph test, so I made arrangements for the test with an operator who was also an instructor at the Minnesota State Crime Bureau.

The suspect showed up for the polygraph test. Of course, he continued to deny any involvement in the crime, yet he utterly failed the test. The polygraph operator told me I had the right person, but the results of the polygraph test itself cannot be used in court against someone. The operator went on to say he was going to keep the test, as it was a classic textbook example of someone trying to fool the machine. The results were so definitive that he said he was going to use it in his instruction of future operators.

While I knew who committed the burglary, I could never clear this case. Sometime later, the suspect's mother came to me and asked what would happen to her son if he continued on his present course of stealing and lying. I told her either he would end up in prison or someone would kill him. Many of his friends did not like him because he kept stealing even from them, and he could never tell a straight story.

Before something terrible could happen to him, he enlisted in the Navy. I learned that he had jumped ship and had gone AWOL (Away With Out Leave) somewhere in Europe. He made his way back to the United States, was picked up by the military police, and wound up in a military prison.

Tongues

When many people hear of the gift of tongues, they automatically think of the Pentecostal denomination or a group of charismatic Christians. The gift of tongues is no doubt the most identifiable of the spiritual gifts, and also the most misunderstood. The gift of tongues can be either in a "known" human language, other than the one spoken by the speaker, or it can manifest as an "unknown or heavenly" language. The apostle Paul wrote, "If I speak with the tongues of men and of angels, but do not have love, I have become a noisy gong or a clanging cymbal" (1 Corinthians 13:1 NASB). What Paul is saying is that if we speak in either a known language or a heavenly language, but that speaking is not done in love, it is heard as just a meaningless noise.

We all possess natural, God-given abilities. Some people are great musicians, while others have amazing abilities in other fields such as math, science, carpentry, or cooking. But these abilities are not *gifts* per se.

I have a friend who was a linguist. He could read, write, and speak Chinese, Korean, Japanese, and he could even manage some Hebrew. He had natural ability for languages, but he did not have the gift of tongues as the Bible uses it. For my friend, his mastery of language was a learned skill. For a spiritual gift to truly be a gift, the speaker has no knowledge or training in the language in which he or she is speaking.

I had a minister friend who was cleaning his apartment one day. As he cleaned, he was praising God out loud. There was a knock on his door. A woman passing by had heard him, and had to find out if he was Portuguese. He told her no, and she asked where he learned to speak Portuguese so beautifully. He had never studied the Portuguese language; he was just praising the Lord in tongues.

There has been much written on this topic, but what is still misunderstood by many is that the gift of tongues is broken down into two distinct functions. The first function for tongues is to be used in one's own prayer time. The second function is for use in a corporate or worship setting. The apostle Paul draws a distinction between personal use and corporate worship in this way:

> For one who speaks in a tongue does not speak to men, but to God; for no one understands, but in his spirit he speaks mysteries...One who speaks in a tongue edifies himself; but one who prophesies edifies the church. Now I wish that you all spoke in tongues, but even more that you would prophesy; and greater is one who prophesies than one who speaks in tongues, unless he interprets, so that the church may receive edifying.
>
> —1 Corinthians 14:2, 4-5 (NASB)

Scripture demands that in the worship setting with a group of people, if someone speaks in tongues, there must be an interpretation of the tongue so that the whole body of Christ may be edified.

Tongues can be and most definitely are used in our own private prayer time. The majority of 1 Corinthians chapter fourteen is on the subject of tongues. In this chapter, the apostle Paul tells us to desire earnestly to prophesy, but never to forbid speaking in tongues. Above all, everything must be done properly and in order.

I have already written about one of my experiences with the gift of tongues that happened during the time of my Christian conversion. Another experience I will reveal later when we consider the gift of miracles.

Interpretation of Tongues

This gift is probably the easiest to understand of all the spiritual gifts. The interpretation of tongues is having the ability to understand and translate the message that has just been spoken in an unknown language. Except through the Holy Spirit, the interpreter does not necessarily know the foreign or heavenly language being spoken.

Recently I was having lunch with my wife and a very dear sister in Christ. The topic of tongues and interpretation of tongues came up when our friend asked me this question: "How do you know if what is interpreted is what God is really saying? If the speaker has no idea what he said, how do you know if the interpretation is correct?"

The Scriptures are very clear on this matter, and they give us two ways of judging whether words spoken are in fact from God. The first way of judging is to:

> Let two or three prophets speak, and let the others pass judgment. But if a revelation is made to another who is seated, let the first keep silent. For you can all prophesy one by one, so that all may learn and all may be exhorted.
>
> —1 Corinthians 14:29-31 (NASB)

Dake's Annotated Reference Bible states that "prophets are also to speak two or three messages in turn, letting others judge whether or not they have spoken truth. Both kinds of messages (tongues and prophecy) are to be judged as to their truth. The basis of judgment is the written revelation of God. If any message in tongues or prophecy does not harmonize with the Bible, or does not come to pass, then it is to be judged false and the person said to be speaking by his own spirit."

The second way of judging is found in the book of James:

> But the wisdom from above is first pure, then peaceable, gentle, reasonable, full of mercy and good fruits, unwavering, without hypocrisy.
>
> —James 3:17 (NASB)

I refer to this verse from James as "the final filter." If a word, an action, or an item reported to be of God can be put through this verse, and if it comes out the same as it went in, then it is of God. If it does not, then discard it.

The proof that any word in tongues or prophecy is from God, whether foretelling or forth-telling, is in its occurrence. If the word happens, then it is truth. If it does not come to pass, then it was of the person, and that person was not operating in the gift from God.

Gifts will sometimes be used in combinations, as I mentioned earlier. For example, I have often seen knowledge and wisdom used in combination, as well as tongues and prophecy. I was attending a Bible study sometime after receiving the spiritual gifts. During a time of prayer, one of the attendees broke into tongues. When she finished, the group was silent. This gift was still new to me, but I understood what the woman said, yet I said nothing. One of the other attendees had also received the interpretation and gave it.

Later, as I was asking God for forgiveness for not giving the interpretation, I tried to justify it by telling him that this was new to me, and I didn't want to be wrong. The Lord told me He forgave me, but revealed that this next Sunday He was going to use me to interpret a word that was going to come forth. In the Bible study group, there were maybe ten people present, but at church there would be six hundred to eight hundred people. Oh boy!

Sunday came. During the time of worship and praise, tongues came forth. The time the tongues were exercised was very lengthy. The congregation grew quiet. Then the Holy Spirit began speaking and giving the interpretation through me. I will never forget what was said. "My children, be at peace and know that I am God. I am the God of Abraham, Isaac, and Jacob. I am He who walked with the three in the fiery furnace. I am He who opened the waters and allowed the children of Israel to pass through the Red Sea on dry ground, and I am He who shut the lion's mouth before Daniel. Are your trials so hot that I cannot cool the fire? Are your troubles so deep that I cannot part them and bring you through on dry ground? And are the accusations against you so fierce that I cannot shut the mouth of the accuser? Be strong my children, and rest in me says the Lord." There was edification, exhortation, and comfort. I have to tell you that I was very shaken after the Lord spoke through me.

The gifts of inspiration are very powerful. It is wonderful knowing that God, through the Holy Spirit, still speaks to us and is willing to use us. It is wonderful that God is so caring for us that He reveals His presence through these gifts. It reinforces the fact that in Christ we are the children of God, the Most High.

CHAPTER SEVEN

GIFTS OF POWER

Faith

Now faith is the assurance of things hoped for, the conviction of things not seen.

—Hebrews 11:1 (NASB)

THE GIFT OF faith is the supernatural ability to believe God without human doubt, unbelief, or reasoning. This is not blind faith, because blind faith is feeling one's way with no guiding light. King David wrote in the book of Psalms that "Thy word is a lamp to my feet, and a light to my path" (119:105 NASB). The gift of faith is a gift of supernatural faith, a faith beyond one's self.

Some years ago Doug Oldham, a Christian recording artist, sang a song that started out, "God said it, and I believe it, and that settles it for me." As a matter of fact, this is my approach to faith. If something is in the Bible, then God said it. If God said something back in Bible days, remembering that Scripture clearly states that the Lord does not change, then God says the same thing today. The Word of God never changes.

Jesus Christ is the same yesterday and today, yes and forever.

—Hebrews 13:8 (NASB)

Every good gift and every perfect gift is from above, and cometh down from the Father of lights, with whom is no variableness, neither shadow of turning.

—James 1:17 KJV

The following stories deal with speaking some things in faith and, while not knowing what the outcome will be, trusting that God will work in them and receive glory from them. My grandmother, Carrie Pendell Clarkson, penned a poem in 1930 that she entitled "Faith." I never had the pleasure of meeting her, but if her children are any measure of her relationship with the Lord, she was a great woman of faith.

FAITH

I hold it true that faith is sight;
'Tis not just blindly groping.
Faith is walking in the light;
Faith is more than hoping.
"Faith is substance of things hoped for,"
Created by thought and prayer;
Gathered from out the ethereal store
That's ever waiting there.
"Faith is evidence of things"
As yet not manifest
Faith is buoyant, borne on wings,
Above the world's unrest.
Faith is visioning desire,
As in a mirror clear;
Warmed by emotion, fanned to fire—
Faith feels and sees and hears.
"Faith is like the mustard seed,"
A mystery enfolding.
It follows a law that all may read—
The law of Faith unfolding.

In the seed is a thought and a plan,
And life, and the urge to grow;
Thus God seeks through seed to man
The Law of Faith to show.
But Faith, like the seed, a promise holds
Of desires fulfilled in fact;
But Faith alone cannot unfold
Unless through Works faith act.

—Carrie Pendell Clarkson

THE OLYMPIC WEIGHT LIFTER

Some years ago I was assisting a deputy sheriff in a traffic stop. The driver of the vehicle was under the influence of alcohol and he became very combative with both the deputy and me. The deputy had done a roadside sobriety test, which the man failed. There was another passenger in the car who was sitting very quietly.

As the deputy attempted to place the driver under arrest, the man grabbed him in a cross-handed choke hold. This sort of hold is very painful, as the person applying the hold works the fingers between the neck muscles and the throat, and then touches the fingertips behind the larynx. He lifted the deputy off the ground, leaving him literally hanging by the neck. This is a martial arts move, and I knew the countermove to it.

I took my flashlight and, in a vertical move, thrust it up between the driver's wrists so he could not rip the deputy's throat out. I then struck the suspect firmly on the base of the jaw. This move really irritated him. It caused him to release that hold, but then he used his right hand to hang the deputy (his feet were about six inches off the ground) and struck me in the chest with his left fist. The kinetic energy was absorbed by my ballistic vest, but the hit was so great it popped a screw out of my glasses and they went in three different directions.

As I picked myself up from the ground, I saw that the deputy had been released from the suspect's hold and was walking back toward his squad car choking and gasping for air. I notified dispatch that I needed a lot of backup. As I radioed my request, the suspect said, "I'm going to spread your guts all over the roadway."

I responded to him by saying, "Neil, you are by far the strongest man I have ever encountered. You should be aware that there is back-up on the way."

He asked if the entire department was coming, and I said yes. As he leaned back against his car, folding his arms across his chest, he said, "Good, I'll wait."

I considered shooting him at one point, but I concluded that would only irritate him. I really didn't think my ammunition would bring him down. Neil was a massive man who stood over six feet tall and weighed in the area of two hundred and fifty pounds.

It finally took approximately ten officers to subdue and restrain him. He was exceedingly strong. When I placed my handcuffs on him, I had to use both hands to close each cuff around his wrists. And I could only get one tooth on each cuff to hold. What I found out later was that Neil had been dismissed from the United States Olympic Weight Lifting Team because he had been in one of the state mental institutions for a number of years.

But this story is not really about Neil; he was arrested and went to jail. The story is more about his passenger and Neil's dog.

It became my responsibility to impound this man's vehicle. We were not going to allow the passenger to leave the scene with the vehicle, as he had also been drinking. As I approached the car, the passenger, who was standing outside of the vehicle, advised me that the dog in the car had the same disposition as the driver. I asked for the dog's name, and I was told it was Fox. Fox was a full-grown German shepherd who did not, at first, appear to like men in uniforms. He did a lot of barking, snarling, and other dog antics to let me know I was not to come any closer to the car.

But I needed to get into the car to inventory it. As I approached the vehicle's driver door, I looked at Fox and in a gentle voice said, "Fox, eirene." The word *eirene* in the Greek means "to be in a harmonious relationship." When I said this, Fox jumped from the front seat into the back seat and then up onto the rear window deck. He kept snarling, though.

I then said, "I guess you didn't hear what I said. In the name of Jesus, be at peace." Fox put his head down and was quiet, allowing me to get fully into the front and back seats to do the work I needed to do. When I finished, I told the passenger that I would be willing to give him a ride to a phone so he could make transportation arrangements.

As we drove toward a restaurant, he asked me what it was I said to the dog. He had never seen anyone, especially a stranger, get anywhere near that dog or his owner's property without a hassle. In that very short ride, I was able to give the man the entire plan of salvation. I explained that in Jesus Christ we have salvation, but we also have the power of the Holy Spirit working through us for the glory of God.

This sort of thing has happened on a number of occasions. I have used the gift of faith for many other situations. So often we are shy about using these gifts, especially outside of the church, because we are not sure how those around us will respond. My counsel is to be bold. Do it. God works through His children when we make ourselves available through the gifts He bestows, and when He does, it will be an opening to witness of Jesus' love for the world.

FROM DEATH TO LIFE

Mik Sen was a man I knew back in the 1970's and 1980's. He worked as a computer guru at one of the local banks, and we attended the same church in Minneapolis. He is a really neat brother in the Lord. It was about Christmas time and Mik had just returned from a men's church retreat. As he was driving home, his car broke down. He was outside his car on the side of the road, looking at the engine, when a motorist struck him and kept on going.

It was after 6:00 P.M. when the call came out, and by this time it was after dark. The accident was about one mile out of my jurisdiction, but I was close to that area. An officer from another city was close by, and he also responded. I was the first on the scene, and as I pulled in I could see Mik's boots still beside his car. He was struck so hard and fast that he was literally knocked out of his boots. He had been thrown from the driver's side of his car into the snowy ditch about thirty feet away, where he had landed on his back.

When I got to Mik he was so badly injured that I did not recognize him. I checked for vital signs right away and found none. The second officer joined me, and he also could not find any life signs. He told me he would cancel the ambulance and instead call the medical examiner, yet as he exited the ditch, the ambulance was pulling up. The paramedics got out but were told the subject was DOA (dead on arrival). They started to get back into their rig, when I yelled, "We have life down here!" I had just prayed and commanded life, in Jesus' name, back into Mik's body. I didn't know if it had happened or not, but I was acting on faith, "the substance of things hoped for, the evidence of things not seen" (Hebrews 11:1 KJV). In other words, I prayed and acted. Jesus commanded life back into Lazarus, Elijah raised the widow's son, the man in the book of Acts who fell out of the window was restored. So why not Mik?

Do I believe Mik was dead? Yes, I do! Do I believe God raised him up again? Yes! In 1979, Jesus People Church in Minneapolis released a musical written by John Worre entitled *The Wind Is Alive*. In this musical, which was performed in hundreds of churches around the nation, Mik gives testimony to this event:

> One evening, not long ago, I was standing by the side of the road and was struck by a hit-and-run driver. I was thrown through the air to land in a heap of broken flesh and bone. I was literally dead at the scene, but the policeman who was the first at my side was a Spirit-filled Christian. Inspired by the Holy Spirit, he commanded life to return to my body. The doctor said I might not come out of the coma, or at best survive as a vegetable or a hopeless cripple. But God, in His mercy and love, is doing today what He did in the book of Acts. Jesus never changes, and I am living proof of His ability not only to heal and restore, but even to bring back life to a lifeless body. Praise the wonderful name of Jesus.[3]

After initial evaluation in the hospital, Mik's family was told by doctors that if he ever regained consciousness, his mental functioning would be severely impaired as he had sustained massive head trauma. But when Mik woke up in the hospital, he did some trouble-shooting on the bank's computer system over the phone.

Healings

Healings is another gift that is somewhat misunderstood. When we think of healing, we often think only of physical healing. But a close look at 1 Corinthians 12:9 and again in 1 Corinthians 12:28 will show that the word *gifts* are used in the plural. This is one gift that goes beyond what we normally think. Beyond the physical, there are psychological and spiritual healings. The gifts of healings will sometimes be used alongside the gift of faith, or the gift of miracles. It is even difficult at times knowing if a healing was not really a miracle, or maybe the result of the gift of faith. In any case, God, through His Holy Spirit, is always the One doing the healing. The Scriptures give definite steps believers can follow for healing:

Is anyone among you sick? Let him call for the elders of the church, and let them pray over him, anointing him with oil in the name of the Lord; and the prayer offered in faith will restore the one who is sick, and the Lord will raise him up, and if he has committed sins, they will be forgiven him. Therefore, confess your sins to one another, and pray for one another, so that you may be healed. The effective prayer of a righteous man can accomplish much.

—James 5:14-16 (NASB)

James declares that anyone who prays for healing, having followed these steps, will be healed. If this is true, then why do some die? I believe that God is sovereign. If a person is healed, it is because God healed him or her. If this person is not healed, then did God become a respecter of persons? The apostle Paul was afflicted with an aliment and asked God to heal him three times:

And because of the surpassing greatness of the revelations, for this reason, to keep me from exalting myself, there was given me a thorn in the flesh, a messenger of Satan to buffet me— to keep me from exalting myself! Concerning this I entreated the Lord three times that it might depart from me. And He has said to me, "My grace is sufficient for you, for power is perfected in weakness." Most gladly, therefore, I will rather boast about my weaknesses, that the power of Christ may dwell in me.

—2 Corinthians 12:7-9 (NASB)

Paul was not healed physically, but he found God's grace to be enough. The Bible says God is not a respecter of persons:

> Then Peter opened his mouth, and said, Of a truth I perceive that God is no respecter of persons: But in every nation he that feareth him, and worketh righteousness, is accepted with him.

> —Acts 10:34-35 (KJV)

Then what happened to Paul and others who were not healed? I have been asked this question many times, and this is what I say: I believe the most perfect healing any believer can receive is to leave this present body and go into the presence of the Lord. The apostle Paul himself said, "we are of good courage, I say, and prefer rather to be absent from the body and to be at home with the Lord" (2 Corinthians 5:8 NASB).

I further believe this life we have been given is to reflect God's glory, not our own. This life is not really about us; it is about the Lord. We are simply His workmanship, so if God chooses to do a healing in or through us, it is for His glory, not ours.

The Scriptures say that it is appointed unto man once to die, and then comes the judgment. We know that in the end, everyone will be resurrected, and in that resurrection all believers will receive a prefect, incorruptible, and glorified body.

The gift of healings, body, soul, and spirit, is supernatural healing power given by the Holy Spirit to a believer to cure all manner of sickness, without human aid or medicine, acting as a liaison, through whom it pleases God to restore health apart from the use of natural means.

A NEW HEART

After moving to Arizona, I received a phone call from my oldest daughter Erica. She was calling to ask if she could also move out to Arizona and move in with us until she could get on her feet. I asked how she was going to get to the Southwest, and she said she would drive. As far as a father is concerned, traveling alone from Minnesota to Arizona in the winter is not a good idea for a daughter. I told her I would fly to Minnesota, and then the two of us would drive back to Arizona together.

As you will learn later in the book, I left law enforcement in December of 1985 due to injuries. In 1989 the family and I moved to Arizona. I moved to the Phoenix area with a job but in December of that same year, I was terminated from my job because I would not falsify documents. Today, that company and its parent company have gone out of business.

I was unemployed at this point, and I really did not have the money to fly. I talked to my pastor at church and explained the situation to him. He put me in touch with a member of the congregation who was working for an airline. This brother in the Lord gave me a "buddy pass" that would take me as far as Chicago. The airline he worked for did not fly into Minneapolis at that time. Then after the church service on the Sunday before I was to leave, a couple came to me and said, "The Lord instructed us to give you sixty-five dollars. We don't know why, but we don't want to be disobedient." That was exactly the cost of a plane ticket from Chicago to Minneapolis. Once again, God provided for my need.

Upon my arrival in Minneapolis, Erica informed me that a friend of hers (and a man I had arrested on a number of occasions) was in the VA hospital after having had numerous heart attacks. She told me the doctors couldn't get the attacks to stop, and that over two-thirds of his heart was now dead.

I asked her to drive me to the VA hospital. Mark was in the Intensive Coronary Care Unit. I found his room and entered. None of the nurses stopped me. In fact, they acted like they hadn't even seen me.

Mark seemed happy for my visit, but he told me he was dying. He explained that all of the tests and instruments were telling the doctors that his heart was failing and there was really nothing they could do for him until the assaults stopped. The problem was the doctors could not get them to stop.

I asked Mark if I could pray for him and ask God to give him a new heart. He asked, "Gregg, do you know how many ministers I have chased out of here?" My response was, "Mark, did you ever know me to run from you?" He admitted I never did. So he told me to go ahead and pray if that was going to make me feel better. I told him I was not doing this for my benefit, but for his. I prayed and asked that the Lord would literally give him a new heart. I then wished him well and left.

I have not seen Mark since the day I prayed for him. I did hear later from my daughter that Mark was released from the hospital the next day after the doctors found absolutely nothing wrong with his heart. In fact, he was told it was as if he had a new heart. Mark was an over-the-road trucker and when he was released from the hospital, he took a Department of Transportation physical to retain his commercial driver's license. He passed it without any problems. Again, to God be the glory.

Child in Seizures

When I was on patrol, I was called to a number of medical and accident scenes. Around the Lake Minnetonka area, I was known as the officer who prays with people at such times. I was called to a residence where a child was having seizures. It was a grand mal seizure (a severe kind of epilepsy) and the parents were having a very difficult time with this one. I requested an ambulance before arriving at the scene.

When I arrived, the boy's mother and father were there, and they were not sure what was happening. I laid my hands on the child and began to pray. Instantly, the seizure stopped. The parents said they knew it was the prayer that stopped the child's seizure. I suggested they take their son to the hospital to be checked by medical personnel anyway. The child, who is now a man about thirty years old, has never had another seizure.

Man Having a Heart Attack

My partner and I received a call of a possible heart attack at the local American Legion Club. We found the man passed out on the floor. People were trying to help by administering CPR.

My partner Curt and I set up the oxygen. He was going to administer the oxygen while I did the chest compressions. Curt gave the man a burst of oxygen and as I put my hands on his chest, I simply said, "In Jesus' name." The man immediately responded. The ambulance arrived, and after a couple of days in the hospital, the man was released in good shape.

A number of the Legionnaires asked what I had done that they had not. One man actually called it a miracle. He said, "Gregg, I've seen death before, and that man was dead when you and Curt arrived. When you put your hands on him, he came back." This incident became a potent witness for the power of the Lord.

My Daughter Erica

There was a teaching going through the churches saying one needed olive oil in order to do healing properly. I actually knew people who kept a bottle of olive oil in their medicine cabinet. In fact, I was one of those people.

One day my daughter Erica came home from school complaining that her leg hurt. She had done something to it. It was reddened and there was dramatic swelling. I went for the medicine cabinet to get my bottle of oil, and on my way there, I asked my daughter Amy if she wanted to pray over Erica with us. Amy was only about three years old at the time.

As I was entering the bathroom to get the olive oil, Amy was entering Erica's room. I then heard, "Jesus, please heal Erica's leg, in Jesus' name, Amen." Amy had taken the lead, and before I could get there, Erica's leg was healed. The redness was gone and so was the swelling. Erica was back on her feet and feeling fine.

Every gift of the Holy Spirit is for use in the body of Christ, the Church. But I have also looked at gifts as God's advertising because I believe there is evidence in the Scriptures for the use of the gifts outside of the Church. However they are used, they are possible due to the Holy Spirit's working power behind them. God brings the result, and it is God who receives the glory through his son, Jesus Christ.

Miracles

We in Western culture need to be very careful when viewing the gift of miracles. Because of a scientific and rationalistic mind-set, a philosophy many have made into a god, miracles are not really considered miracles but rather the result of some other action of nature. Our understanding of science and nature is still a mystery, and that is true in every avenue of learning. We know a lot, and God has given medical science much knowledge on how to cure diseases, but we still don't have a full understanding. According to C. Peter Wagner, the gift of miracles is "the ability that God gives to certain members of the Body of Christ to serve as human intermediaries through whom it pleases God to perform powerful acts that are perceived by observers to have altered the ordinary course of nature."[4]

THE TORNADO

I was teaching a college-age Bible study in the early 1980s for a group attending an Evangelical Free Church. For the most part, at that time, the church did not accept the charismatic gifts or any teaching that the Holy Spirit's miraculous gifts are relevant for today. We were meeting at one of the member's apartment in Wayzata. The apartment complex was located on a rise, so from the top floor one could see much of the city and areas west of the city. We were studying J.I. Packer's *Knowing God*. It is an excellent and famous book. When we finished the chapter on the Holy Spirit, I asked the group if they were satisfied with what we had studied. Most said they were. I then asked, "How then do we obtain the power that the Holy Spirit has to give?"

One of the attendees sarcastically came back with, "Here we go, the baptism of the Holy Spirit." Packer had not covered this topic, but everyone in the group seemed to have preconceived ideas of what this was. For the most part, they wanted nothing to do with this because it was labeled in their minds as "charismatic." Another person asked, "What is it you believe you have in the baptism of the Holy Spirit that I don't have in the name of Jesus?" This really is a very good question. My response was, "power to witness for Jesus." He agreed that he was lacking in this area.

As the study was drawing to a close, tornado sirens began to blow. We went out on the balcony of the apartment and could see a tornado, still some distance away, coming in our direction. It was on the ground and not doing much damage to the open area, but it was approaching a residential area. When I pointed at the funnel cloud and commanded in the name of Jesus that it return to the clouds from whence it came, it immediately did.

Would the tornado have gone back into the clouds anyway? Did this command alter the course of nature? Was it just perfect timing? I still don't have a full understanding of tornados and how they act, but I believe that the course of nature was altered. I know this event had a tremendous effect on those at the Bible study, and I know it continued to build my faith. As with any gift, if there is a resultant effect it is because God chose to do something at that point in time. If not, He chose not to. Again, God was advertising, and those at the Bible study now wanted to know more about the power of the Holy Spirit.

THE MOTORCYCLE AND AMY'S BIRTH

October 4, 1974, was my first experience with the active power of the Holy Spirit's gifts. It had only been about two months since I came to Jesus Christ, so everything dealing with true Christianity was still very new to me. My daughter, Amy, was about to make her debut into the world and I was at work when I got the phone call that it was time to go to the hospital.

In October of 1974, however, there was a gas shortage. The gas stations closed at about 7:00 P.M., and this call came in after the stations had closed. I was riding my motorcycle and headed for home. I got to the Wayzata city limits when my engine informed me that it was out of gas. I had about thirty miles to go, so I switched to the reserve tank. I prayed that the Lord would get me home, although thirty miles was farther than my reserve tank would take me. After about ten miles, the sound of the engine changed from a combustion sound to a whirring sound. In any event, I made it home, got my wife into the car, and we went to the hospital.

The labor was long and hard. Seventeen hours later, our baby girl was born. We named her "Amy Joy," after the first two elements of the fruit of the Holy Spirit, love and joy. After Amy's birth, I was really tired, so I went home for some rest. My wife needed her rest also. About an hour later, I received a call from my wife saying that I needed to return to the hospital right away. Amy was very ill and overheating. The hospital personnel were not sure she was going to live. I hurried back to the hospital, praying all the way.

Before I got there, a specialist had been called in to attend to Amy. He was rather annoyed because he had been called away from a dinner party. A nurse had wrapped Amy in a blanket and placed her in a heated isolette. The doctor turned off the isolette and removed the blanket from her. She cooled down right away.

That night I called a friend of mine who worked at KTIS radio. I told him of Amy's birth and then filed a praise report. He told me to listen to the radio. About fifteen minutes later he played "Because He Lives" by Bill and Gloria Gaither and dedicated this song to Amy.

Car in the Ditch

The winter of 1974-75 was a very snowy one. One evening while on patrol, I came across a vehicle that had slid off the road and was completely stuck in the median between westbound Highway 12 and the north service road. The snow was really piled up around the car. I turned my lights on and pulled over to assist. A lady and her son were outside of the vehicle. As I approached, she said, "I guess the normal thing to do is to call a tow truck." I said, "Yeah, that would be the normal thing to do, but I'm not a normal cop." I wish I could describe the look on her face when she heard that statement.

Things were about to get more interesting as my mind recalled a specific verse:

> And He said to them, "Because of the littleness of your faith; for truly I say to you, if you have faith as a mustard seed, you shall say to this mountain, 'Move from here to there,' and it shall move; and nothing shall be impossible to you."
>
> —Matthew 17:20 (NASB)

A car is not a mountain, so I believed this should be pretty easy. I instructed the woman to get back into her car and told her that when I yell, "Now!" she should put constant pressure on the gas pedal but not spin the tires. I asked her son to join me at the rear of the vehicle, and help me push the car out of the ditch.

The boy and I went to the rear of the car and placed our hands on the trunk lid. I then said, "Car, in the name of Jesus, get out of this ditch… now!" As the car moved effortlessly out of the ditch, both her son and I wound up face down in the snow. As I got up and was brushing the snow off, the son had run over to his mother and was telling her what had happened at the rear of the car. She looked even more astonished than before and said, "Whoever or whatever you are, thank you." I simply told her to praise the Lord, have a good night, and to please drive safely. I returned to my squad car and left.

My First Injury Accident

On June 20, 1977, I was working the middle shift and got off at about 10:00 P.M. I went home, reviewed my day with my wife, and went to bed. That night, I could not get to sleep. I felt something exciting in my spirit, but I couldn't put my finger on what was happening. I got out of bed and told my wife I was going for a walk.

I went to an all-night gas station and superette. A young man who I had come to know was working and we began to talk about spiritual things. I asked Paul if he was a Christian. He said he was not. I asked if he had any idea of what was going to happen to him when he died. Then I explained that according to the Bible, when a person dies, he goes directly into the presence of the Lord. Paul told me that before he died, he would have time to repent, but he was not ready to do that quite yet. I told him God was going to do something the next day that was really exciting, but I didn't know what it was that he was going to do. With that, I left and went back home to bed.

The next day was the sunny and warm first day of summer. I went to work at 2:00 P.M., and it seemed it was going to be a normal shift. It turned out to be anything but normal. My shift, my life, and all that I thought to be normal ended at about 4:45 P.M.

I received a radio call concerning a property damage accident on County Road 15 near the Woodhill Country Club. I responded to the accident as did an Orono officer and a Hennepin County sheriff's car. When we arrived on the scene, we found that one vehicle headed east had stopped to make a left-hand turn. A trailing vehicle had tried to pass on the right side, but went off the roadway and onto the gravel shoulder.

That vehicle was pulling a flatbed trailer. As he attempted to pass, the trailer bounced on the rough shoulder and clipped the rear end of the vehicle making the left turn. The trailer then bounced off the vehicle, striking a power support pole on the south side of the road. This pole supported a power pole that was on the north side of the road. The support pole was knocked down. So we had two vehicles with damage, a downed pole, and a guide wire from the support pole crossing the roadway. There was also a guide wire still attached to the support pole which was anchored in the ground.

The county car went to the east of the accident scene to slow down west-bound traffic. The Orono officer and I stayed by the pole, trying to figure out the best way to remove the guide wire from the roadway. The guide wire appeared to be touching other wires on the power pole across the road. One of the men involved in the accident reached out to touch the guide wire. He told me later that I probably saved his life when I kicked his hand away from the guide wire. That was the last thing I really remember.

A driver of a vehicle going west was not watching where we were directing her. She drove off the roadway and onto the shoulder of the road. The wire became hooked in that vehicle's right front wheel-well, which started a terrible chain reaction of events.

The pole that was down was being pulled and began to rise up off the ground. As it rose, it struck the people from the first accident, the Orono officer, and me. The first two accident people were basically tripped by the pole. The Orono officer was struck in the back of his legs, and as he began to fall backward, the pole rode up his back, struck the back of his head, and put him on the ground. I was struck in the lower right leg, breaking the non-weight-bearing bone on contact. I was then flipped about fifteen feet through the air. The back of my head and neck landed on the trailer that had originally downed the pole, and the rest of my body went to the ground. The deputy directing traffic said we looked like a bunch of bowling pins that had just been hit. He said we went flying everywhere. This was now an even more serious situation.

The Orono officer sat in the middle of the road, calling for help on his portable radio. The deputy came to our position to give us aid, and he later told me that when he got to me, my eyes were wide open and fixed, and not responding to the sunlight. He went on to say I had no color in my face, and as he bent down to try and get vital signs on me, my bladder let loose. These are classic signs of death.

Believing I was dead, he left me to get a blanket to cover me. The next Orono officer on the scene was not so willing to let me die. Chuck tried CPR, but could not get my chest to compress because I was wearing a ballistic vest. He ripped my shirt open, cut the straps removing the front panel, and did a precortal thump to my sternum. This shocked my heart and got it beating again.

When the paramedics arrived, they did their primary and secondary survey of my body. They believed I had a skull fracture and a broken neck because of the way my head was bent off to one side. And because my chest was like mush, I either had all of my ribs broken, or all of my ribs had separated from the spinal column. As if this was not enough, I also had a broken leg. This was quite an inventory of injuries.

The Wayzata Fire Rescue and North Memorial Hospital ambulance put me on a backboard and totally immobilized me. They placed me in a stiff cervical collar, sandbagged my head and neck, and began the twenty-mile trip to the hospital. Each intersection between the accident scene and the hospital was opened, so the ambulance did not have to slow down.

While all of this was transpiring, my police chief and a representative from the ambulance company went to my house to inform my wife of the accident and transport her to the hospital. The chief assured my wife that I was okay, and he said that the other officer who was injured was not expected to live. He had it backwards. I was the one not expected to live through the first night. In fact, the officers were so certain I would not make it that they outlined my body on the roadway.

In the ambulance I drifted in and out of consciousness. I would wake up and ask a string of questions: "What happened? Is everyone all right? Did anyone get hurt? Oh well, praise the Lord!" Then I would pass out again. I guess I went through this litany of questions so many times that the other officer being transported told me later that if I had said it one more time, it would be one time too many. He said, "If you didn't have a head injury before, I was going to give you one."

Once in the emergency room at North Memorial Hospital, the doctors and nurses began working on me. The x-rays showed I had a broken leg and a massive closed head injury. The good news was my neck was not broken, nor did I have a skull fracture, and all of my ribs seemed fine. The other officer involved was also doing okay. My wife was already at the hospital and his parents were summoned. The other officer's dad was a minister, so there was quite a prayer meeting going on in the waiting room.

Apparently everyone could hear me speaking very loudly when they were in the waiting room. One of the emergency room nurses came out to speak with my wife and the others. She said the reason I was doing so much yelling was that a patient with a head injury can't hear very well. She went on to say that I kept asking the same questions over and over, which was normal for a head-injury patient, but then I would speak some gibberish that no one could understand. My wife told me later that I was speaking in tongues, and when she heard that she knew that I was going to be fine.

Closed head injuries are an interesting study. My wife called a close friend of ours who was a Church of God minister named Reginald Daniels. He was and is a great man of God. He came to the hospital and prayed by my bedside all night. When I would wake up, I knew who he was, but I couldn't figure out who the woman was that was with him. It turned out that it was my wife.

Around 6:00 A.M., I phoned the KTIS radio station. I spoke with the announcer and told him what happened to me. I asked him to play the song, "The Love of Jesus, It won't Stop," and he was gracious enough to play it.

A neurologist came in to see me later in the morning and asked me all the routine questions: "Do you know what day it is? Do you know where you are? Who is the president of the United States? What is your name? What year were you born?" I had the wrong day, had no idea where I was, except I knew that I was in a hospital, I was only two or three presidents behind, and no, I could not tell him my name or date of birth. Then something very interesting happened. I told him I didn't know *who* I was, but I could tell him *Whose* I was. He questioned me on that, and I told him I knew I was a child of God, and I even gave him Scripture to back it up. I think he then thought my head injury was especially bad. I still did not know I was married and had two children. I recognized people I had only met once, but I could not remember those closest to me.

This accident happened on a Monday, and I was released from the hospital on Thursday. A day or so later, I was sitting on my deck when my wife told me I had a visitor. It was Paul from the superette. He stopped by to see how I was doing. During our conversation, I told Paul I was going to pose the same question to him I posed the other night: "When are you going to die?" I went on to tell him that if my life had not been right before the Lord, there was no time from when the pole struck me until I hit the trailer for me to repent. I would have gone into the presence of God unprepared. Death happens quickly sometimes.

Paul dropped immediately to his knees and accepted Jesus as Lord and Savior. There were tears of joy. I have told many people since that day that if this accident brought one more person into the Kingdom, it was all worth it. I was released from the hospital with a diagnosis of dyslexic syndrome, retrograde amnesia, and a broken leg, on which was placed a walking cast. The retrograde amnesia meant the memory banks in my head had basically been erased from the time of the accident back to when I was a child. It took some time for all of this to be healed. It did cause some interesting moments. I knew I was a cop, but I couldn't remember how to *be* a cop. I had forgotten how to perform some of the most basic functions of law enforcement.

When I was back on the job making a traffic stop, I would notify the dispatcher. The problem was that I would turn numbers and letters around on license plates. Sometimes I could not remember why I had stopped the vehicle, so I would ask the driver if he knew why I had stopped him. Whatever answer he gave became the correct one, and I would then warn and release him. The frustration in all of this was that I used to have a near photographic memory. Now, the bump on my head made that a thing of the past.

A sergeant from a neighboring department was a good friend of mine. I told him about the memory problems I was experiencing and asked that he retrain me. I asked that he not reveal my problems and my need for retraining to the administration in my department, and he honored that request. We spent a number of nights going over how to make a DWI (Driving While Intoxicated) arrest, the paperwork involved, how to make a felony stop, and other basics. I was relearning all the basics, and even advancing my training. For example, I later became state certified as both a breathalyzer operator and intoxilyzer operator.

During the next six weeks, I had a lot of time to spend in Scripture and prayer. As I stated earlier, the Lord never does just one thing in any event. I needed to get my memory back and this was accomplished through daily Bible reading.

> He saved us, not on the basis of deeds which we have done in righteousness, but according to His mercy, by the washing of regeneration and renewing by the Holy Spirit.
>
> —Titus 3:5 (NASB)

The Lord was bathing me in His Word, which was bringing about a regeneration of my mind. My memory, for the most part, is now restored, but there are some shadowy areas to this day. God also showed me that there was little enough time left to lift up the name of Jesus and that I should quit being so involved with teaching on Satan and the occult. From that point on, I have seldom discussed those things. When the subject would surface again, I would couch it in Jesus Christ and raise Him up.

As an aside to all of this, when I was in the hospital, an attorney came to see me. The other officer had called the law firm of Schwebel, Getz and Sieben, and the firm wanted to represent us in a suit against the other driver. I had never been involved in this sort of thing before, but I agreed to go forward with it.

On January 1, 1980, it was announced on the television news that my case had been heard in the Supreme Court of Minnesota and I had won. The verdict became a landmark decision. Prior to this, police officers did not have the right to sue for on-duty injury. What is known as the "Fireman's Rule" was always brought up. The idea here is that when there is inherent danger in the job, the potential for injury is always present, so there is no right to sue for injury. The case was argued that there were hidden dangers that could not have been foreseen. Police officers all over the nation now have the right to redress for injury. My case made the law books in the Supreme Court of Minnesota ruling Griffiths v Lovelette Transfer Company. This landmark case has not been limited to just police officers, but has been brought into play in other cases nationwide.

This was the first of two traumatic accidents I experienced. (I will discuss the other later.) At this time in my life, I wanted to leave law enforcement and go into full-time ministry. I had talked it over with my wife, and her comment was, "You aren't in full-time ministry now?" I really wanted to hang up the gun belt, but the Lord had a different plan. I agreed to stay in the police department, and I told God I would not leave until He removed me. Later, He did.

Child Drowning Victim

I was at the police station on a sunny August afternoon when I received a radio call of a child drowning. I raced out of the building and headed for my squad car. Nothing will hurry an officer more than a call involving a child.

As I left the parking lot, I requested that an ambulance be dispatched. I was at the scene in two minutes, which was pretty good time considering I had to clear three major intersections. The mother had the child at the driveway but still on the sidewalk. The child was limp and unconscious. I checked for a pulse and respiration and found a slight pulse but no breathing. I turned the child on his side and pulled his abdomen into my knee cap. At the same time I said, "Breathe in Jesus' name." I heard a cry, and the child vomited. This cleared his airway.

The ambulance arrived and the paramedics started checking the child. They were going to transport. The mother looked at me and said that she had another young son who was on his way home from school. I told her to go with the ambulance and I would wait for the child and take him to my home, where my wife and I would take care of him.

That evening the mother arrived at our home to pick up her son. She said the other child was doing well and that there didn't appear to be any brain damage from the near drowning.

The Wayzata News · Week of Aug. 25, 1980 · Page 3

City commends police officer

Wayzata Police Officer Gregg Griffiths was cited by the Wayzata police department for his actions in saving the life of a young boy earlier this month.

The council officially passed a resolution commending the policeman.

On the afternoon of Aug. 12, Griffiths received a radio call concerning a reported drowning at 250 South Bushaway Road in Wayzata. He arrived on the scene within two minutes and found Mrs. Liann Zenanko attempting to revive her one-year-old son, Garret, with C.P.R. methods. Moments earlier, Mrs. Zenanko had found her son lying face down in the family swimming pool.

Griffiths found that the boy was not breathing and that his pulse was extremely weak. He then turned Garret onto his side and administered light abdominal thrusts which caused the child to vomit, and allowed him to breathe again.

Police Chief David Bruhn said that after talking with Mr. and Mrs. Zenanko and paramedics from North Hospital where Garret was taken later, he was convinced that Griffiths' "swift and effective measures were instrumental in saving the life and preventing serious injury" to the boy.

Garret has been on the Wayzata police force since 1971. This winter he completed an 80-hour Emergency Medical Technicians course for police officers. Bruhn said three of Wayzata's five officers have completed the course. The other two are slated to take the course this fall.

Extension offers classes

Hundreds of University of Minnesota extension classes are scheduled this year for people who want to sharpen job skills and enhance career opportunities through college classes.

Introductory and advanced courses are offered evenings and weekends in accounting, business law, industrial relations, computer science, management, real estate and several other business-related topics. Degrees are available in accounting and business administration, as well as 25 other major study areas, through evening attendance. But students don't have to be in a degree program to take classes.

Registration by mail begins Aug. 25 for fall quarter classes. Call 376-3000 to request the new 1980-81 extension classes bulletin that describes registration procedures, courses and degrees and certificates. Fall classes begin Sept. 29.

Last day to register without a late fee is Sept. 16.

In addition to regular college credit courses, dozens of noncredit courses are scheduled, including over 40 professional improvement courses. These are short-term classes designed for new managers or professional people that feature instructors from the University and the business community. Topics range from computers and communication to vocational planning and sales techniques.

County libraries
set fall hours

Newspaper article on child rescue

RESOLUTION NO. 1996

RESOLUTION COMMENDING OFFICER GREGG GRIFFITHS

WHEREAS, on August 12, 1980, Gregg Griffiths responded in his capacity as Wayzata Police Officer to a call for assistance at 250 S. Bushaway Road; and

WHEREAS, upon arrival Officer Griffiths took action which was instrumental in saving the life and preventing injury to one and a half year old Garret Zenanko who was found near drowning by his mother in the family swimming pool; and

WHEREAS, no greater recognition of a standard of performance is possible for a Wayzata Police Officer than that for action saving the life of a child;

NOW BE IT RESOLVED by the City Council of the City of Wayzata, Minnesota, that Officer Gregg Griffiths be recognized and commended for his actions of August 12, 1980 as serving in the highest degree the citizens of the community by saving the life of a child.

BE IT FURTHER RESOLVED that Officer Griffiths be presented with a copy of this Resolution as appropriate recognition of his actions.

Adopted by the Wayzata City Council this 19th day of August, 1980.

Mayor

ATTEST:

City Manager

City Citation

CITY OF WAYZATA

800 RICE STREET, WAYZATA, MINN. 5839
PHONE 473-023

August 18, 1980

Gregg Evan Griffiths
Police Officer
Wayzata Police Department

SUBJECT: Departmental Commendation

At approximately 3:08 p.m. on August 12, 1980 you received a radio call
concerning a reported drowning at 250 South Bushaway Road in the City of
Wayzata. You arrived on the scene within two minutes and found Mrs. Liane
Zenanko doing C.P.R. on her son (Garret Zenanko 1½ years), and was advised
by Mrs. Zenanko that she had found her son lying face down in the family
swimming pool. You quickly checked and found the boys pulse was weak and
no air exchange was taking place. At that time you turned the boy on his
side and administered light abdominal thrusts which caused the child to vomit,
thus clearing the airway and allowing him to breathe. Oxygen was
administered and North Ambulance arrived on the scene and transported
Garret Zenanko to the hospital.

After talking with Mr. and Mrs. Zenanko and the paramedics from North
Hospital, I am convinced that your swift and effective measures were
instrumental in saving the life and preventing serious injury to Garret
Zenanko.

Your actions were in the highest tradition of law enforcement and you are to
be commended for a job well done. I can think of no greater achievement for
a Law Enforcement Officer and rest assured that your actions have brought
credit not only to yourself, but your department as well.

Please accept my thanks and congratulations for a job well done.

Sincerely,

David A. Brehm
Chief of Police
Wayzata Police Department

Police Department Commendation

MY SECOND ACCIDENT

February 1, 1985, was a life-changing day. It was about −14 degrees
and sunny. An officer from the Mound Police Department had phoned
my PD. He was off duty and his vehicle would not start. He was at a
shopping center in my patrol area and called to ask for assistance in

getting his car started. I told him I would be right there to help. I never made it.

As I was traveling west on County Road 15, I started to cross the Arcola Bridge. A vehicle going east was crossing the bridge from the other end. He saw me and thought I had him on radar, so he slammed on his brakes. He didn't realize he was on black ice. His vehicle skidded and was coming over the center line right at me. He was driving a late 1970s Honda Accord and I was in a 1984 Ford Crown Victoria. I had nowhere to go to avoid the collision. Just prior to our impact, his vehicle turned a little to my right. The impact tore his car into two pieces. Everything from the steering wheel forward went one direction, and the cab and the rest of the vehicle went another.

Minnesota did not have a seat-belt law at the time and I refused to wear mine. I am left-handed, and thus I wore my weapon on my left hip. When the seat belt would retract, it normally got hung up on my weapon. More than once I was spun to the ground getting out of my vehicle in a hurry. My being left-handed plays a part in this story.

As we collided, I was thrown forward in my seat, hitting the steering wheel with my chest. My left shoulder was caught between the steering wheel and the spotlight handle. My right knee went into the radio stack, and my face careened off the top of the steering wheel and went into the windshield. I was certain my vehicle was going to go through the bridge rails and down about thirty feet to the ice below. I pushed myself off the steering wheel and leaned over on my right side to prepare for the impact with the ice. Thankfully, my squad car stayed on the bridge deck.

From my position on the front seat, I radioed in the accident. It went something like this:

Me: "6521 Emergency!"
Dispatcher: "6521, go ahead."
Me: "6521, I've been hit. (with difficulty breathing) Need backup and an ambulance."
Dispatcher: "What is your location?"
Me: "I'm on the Arcola Bridge, County Road 15."

What I learned later was that other officers thought I had been shot. One officer was in his office sitting at his desk. He did not go around it but vaulted over it as he left his office to come to my aid.

Some years earlier I had taken a street survival course so I put a lot of that training into practice right then. I kept repeating that I was not going to die. I knew I was badly broken up inside, as I could taste blood in my mouth, and I could smell blood in my airway. I also prayed. I wanted to make sure that I was forgiven for everything, just in case I did go into the presence of the Lord. Instead, God's presence came into mine.

A man opened the passenger door and informed me that my squad car was on fire and said he needed to pull me out. Remember I said I was left-handed? I was lying on my right side, which meant my weapon was available to me. I was concentrating on the radio, trying to control the pain in my chest. I told the man that if he touched me, I would shoot him where he stood. So many times, good Samaritans do more damage to the victim while trying to rescue them in a panic. I knew that if I stayed still, I would be fine.

I asked the man if he actually saw flames. He told me no, and said he just saw a lot of smoke. I figured that at −14 degrees, with a smashed radiator and probably a busted battery, there would be a lot of steam, and that was what he was interpreting as smoke. I pushed the button on the dashboard that opened the trunk and told him there was a fire extinguisher in the trunk. I asked him to use it if he saw flames, but under no circumstances was he to touch me. I never actually saw the man. I kept my eyes on the radio, trying to control my pain. The photos of the accident scene show that the man and our conversation was real; I had not hallucinated, as the trunk lid is open and the fire extinguisher is out of the trunk and on the ground.

Next there was a female voice saying, "Let me through, let me through!" The passenger door opened, and a female sat on the remaining portion of the front seat. She asked, "Officer, what is your name?" I told her. She then asked, "Where do you hurt?" I told her, "Center chest." She very gently placed one hand on my head and her other hand on my chest. She then started praying.

I said, "Ma'am, this is the ministry I need right now. What is your name?" She did not answer but broke into tongues praying. I again thanked her and asked her name. Still she did not answer but started to travail (travailing is an agonizing weeping that sometimes occurs during intercessory prayer). I could feel her tears landing on my head. Again I asked her name. The only response I got was, "Help is arriving, and I'll get out of their way." The door closed and the next thing I heard over the radio was my sergeant saying he was on the accident scene.

The sergeant approached my squad car and looked through the driver's side window that was no longer there, asking how I was. I told him I was busted up inside. I asked how the other driver was and was told he was out of his vehicle walking around. The sergeant then got on his radio and requested the sheriff's crime lab and the Wayzata Fire Rescue "on the red." The only reason we ever requested the crime lab on the red to an accident scene was if death was imminent. The sergeant just told me the other driver was fine, so I concluded I was dying. The mobile crime lab was in the area and got there before the ambulance and fire rescue team. Photos of the accident scene show the driver's side door still on the squad car, with me still inside.

Now, I need to backtrack a little at this point. There was a body shop in our area that was also a chop-shop (a place where parts from stolen cars are stripped and sold). The FBI had an agent in deep cover for about one and a half years in this shop and had put out an "attempt to locate" bulletin on a Honda Accord. Well, I figured out after the collision that I had found it.

After I was extracted from the squad car and put into the ambulance, I was placed into a G suit, or gravity suit, which is used to push blood out of the lower extremities and into the chest cavity. The suit acts like an internal transfusion of blood. It is used mostly to prevent shock and to supply more blood to the chest and brain. As I lay in the ambulance, they were losing me. I was going into shock. The medics could not detect a blood pressure on me, and they had to use a manual method.

The other driver was transported in the same ambulance. I began to talk to him about the goodness and grace of God. He really did not want to hear any of this, so I began talking to him about his vehicle.

At this point, I did not know that it had been torn into two pieces, but somehow I seemed to know that this was the car the FBI wanted.

When I reached the hospital, there was concern as to whether I was going to survive this accident. The same team of doctors that had worked on me back in 1977 was waiting for my arrival.

As I lay in the emergency room, my chief came in to see me. I told him that I found the car the Feds wanted. He said he knew that, but did I have to destroy the squad car to do it? He had joked at the accident scene that they were going to deduct money from my pay check to pay for the damage to the squad. I laughed and told him I didn't think so. He told me later that when he heard me laugh, he knew I would be fine.

The doctors did all sorts of x-rays and blood tests, and then they put me into the Intensive Care Unit (ICU). I had tubes, IVs, and all sorts of equipment hooked up to me monitoring just about everything. At about 5:00 P.M. a chest specialist came in. As he started to talk to me, the local news was just coming on the TV. I asked that he be quiet as I wanted to see the accident scene.

The aerial photo of the bridge looked like a war zone. The doctor just stood there looking at me, the news, and my charts. He was shaking his head. He could not believe I was still alive. He explained to me that if I had not been wearing my ballistic vest with the sternum trauma plate, my aorta would probably have separated from my heart, and I would have bled out inside my chest cavity. As it was, the trauma plate, which is normally a concave shaped armor plate that covers the heart, was flattened out when I hit the steering column, and it broke two of my ribs. The concern the doctors had for me in the emergency room was that one of the broken ribs had either nicked a lung or my heart. Needless to say, the Lord had protected me from all of this.

I was released from the hospital the next morning. I went right from a bed in ICU to the street. This is not normal procedure, to say the very least. What the doctors didn't find at the time, but that was revealed through an MRI two years later, was that my back had been broken in this accident. The x-rays taken in the emergency room did not show that one of the "wings" attaching to the spinal column had been partially broken. It is between these wings that the nerve bundles going to the legs pass through. When the bone healed, the orbit that the nerves pass through became smaller, and thus the bone was rubbing on the nerves every time I would bend or twist. This would cause pain in the lower back. Minneapolis did not get an MRI unit until about 1987. The MRI found the problem.

I was told in 1987 there was nothing medically, surgically, or therapeutically that could be done for me. I was told within ten years I would lose my legs and spend the rest of my life in a wheelchair. At this writing I am twenty-plus years after the fact. My legs are still strong and no wheelchair is in sight. To quote the first phrase of a song by Fanny J. Crosby, "To God be the glory, great things he hath done!"

My wife picked me up from the hospital, and I told her I wanted to go to the PD to see my vehicle. As I walked into the department, the sergeant was on the phone with the hospital. They told him I was doing fine. While that call was going on, I was standing, looking over the top of his cubicle smiling at him. He hung up and told me the hospital still thought I was there. At this point I started questioning him.

I wanted to know who the woman was who got out of my squad car as he arrived at the accident scene. He told me no one got out of my car. I said, "Gary, there was a woman praying over me when you arrived." Again, he said that no one got out of my car. I told him she said he was arriving and that she was going to get out of the way. He repeated that no one was in my car. I then asked if he got the names of the witnesses to the accident. He said he did. I asked to see the list, as I wanted to see who the women were at the scene. His response was, "Gregg, there were no women at the accident scene." I have told this story to a number of minister friends and others, and many of them say I had an angelic visitation. My response has been whether this was a mortal or immortal visitation, there was an obedient servant of the Lord praying over me.

On the Sunday following the accident, I was in a lot of pain. The medication had worn off, and I was finding it difficult to breathe. I was supposed to be teaching a Sunday school class, so I had my wife call the church and tell them we would not be there. We did not mention the problem.

After the church service, one of the ministers phoned and asked if he and some others could come to my home and pray over me. I was in favor of this. He then asked, "What is the problem?" I told him I had been in a traffic accident and I had two broken ribs. He got very excited and said, "Brother, claim your healing! A word of knowledge was spoken in the service during worship and praise. A brother stated that someone in the congregation is being healed of two broken ribs."

A week after the accident, I went for a follow-up x-ray of my chest. I had seen the initial x-rays, and then I saw those taken at this follow-up visit. The original photographs showed a definite break in two ribs, with separation and fragments floating. Those taken a week later showed no evidence of any breaks. In fact, there was not even a calcium heal line, which would have been the normal thing to find. I asked the doctor how he would explain all this and his comeback was, "Ribs heal quickly." Yes, especially when God is the One doing the healing.

This accident resulted in my having to leave law enforcement. This became a time of faith-testing. As I mentioned earlier, the doctors did not discover that my back had been broken until 1987. But even in 1985 they felt my body had been through too much trauma for one lifetime, and they told me that in all good conscience they could not recommend my going back to police work. In fact, one of them was in tears when giving me this news. He knew how much I loved my career. I told him I was still young, intelligent, and creative, and that I knew God had a plan, although I didn't know what it was at that time. That plan is still being worked out in my life today.

All of this put my personal theology to the test. A person can preach and teach all sorts of biblical truths, but until it is tested in one's own life, it is just words. The city would not medically retire me. Because of external factors I could not control, I lost my pension. My family was falling apart, and I had no idea how to stop all of this. Finances were a mess and between my wife and me, we had to work seven part-time jobs. One of my daughters was not handling adolescence well and was a constant runaway, along with the drug scene. Since she wanted to live anywhere but at home, I kicked her out. That is a whole episode in and of itself. I spent many hours studying the book of Job. I really felt I was reliving Job's story. A song recorded by the Sharret Brothers kept coming to mind:

> (Chorus) If, when I'm put through the fire, I'll come out shining like gold; Oh Lord, please don't ever stop working with me 'til you see I can be all you want me to be. I am willing Lord, I am willing Lord, to be just exactly what you want me to be.[5]

God is still not finished with me yet, and I pray He never will be. He has given me an exciting life. The Lord never promises anyone an easy life, but He does promise to go through our trials with us. There is no greater comfort than to know the Lord will never leave us nor forsake us. It really is an awesome thought to know we are daily in the presence of the living God.

The photos on the following pages were taken by the Hennepin County Sheriff's Crime Lab. Deputy Larry Cappeller, who took the photos, still shakes his head today, finding it difficult to believe I lived through this accident. As a crime lab technician, Larry has taken many photos of accident scenes.

Extinguisher by car and trunk lid open

Skid marks on bridge
This photo was shot after I had been taken away in the ambulance.
It shows the skid marks.

Mirror on hood of squad car
This photo shows the paramedic working on me in the car. The interior rearview
mirror on my car's hood belongs to the other vehicle. It stuck to my hood as I
drove through his vehicle.

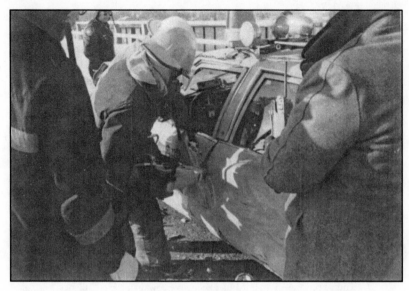

Jaws of Life
Here the Wayzata Fire Rescue is cutting me out of my squad car.

Front half of striking vehicle
This is the front end of the other vehicle. It is truly a miracle the driver survived.

Back half of car
This is the other piece of his car. When he exited his car
he simply stepped forward.

God's hand was on both of us, even though the other driver was not willing to admit it at the time.

CHAPTER EIGHT

POST SCRIPT

Tim's Story

THERE ARE MANY other stories I could tell of strange and wonderful things that have happened in my life. But let me offer a couple more having to do with the gifts as used by others.

In the early eighties, there was an area in the city on Mill Street where some of the rougher youths would gather. They would start gathering around 6:00 P.M. and continue hanging around into the night. These were dopers, thieves, assaulters, and every other sort of potential criminal. My partner Curt and I would do our best to keep an eye on the activity, but many of the shoppers would not go near this area because of these youth gatherings. I knew something had to be done about this but I wasn't sure what.

I was discussing this with my wife one evening, and I told her that these kids needed to be evangelized. I wasn't sure how or where this could be accomplished. She suggested that we have a spaghetti feed at our house, and then have a Bible study afterward. I put the word out on the street that on Thursday evening there would be food and Bible study at my place. The kids could come for just the food, or just the study, or both.

On the first evening, about fifteen kids showed up. They had so much fun they wanted to do it weekly, and they volunteered to bring the food next time. I had to put a condition on this: no stealing to get the food. The study continued for about eighteen months and grew to about forty regular attendees over that time period. Most made decisions for the Lord, and crime went down the tubes in that area of the city.

What I was teaching was practical theology. These kids hadn't had any church background in their lives, and they were very ignorant about Scripture. I had felt for some time, and still do, that unless one's theology is practical and can be used daily, it is just head knowledge and worth nothing. I wanted these people to put into practice what they learned.

There was a young man who came to the study regularly who had been a doper and had assaulted someone. This young man was also living out of his truck, as he had no permanent dwelling. His name was Tim and he was an interesting person.

One Thursday afternoon I was going off duty when the chief called me into his office. He asked if I knew Tim and where Tim was going to be that night. I told him he would be at my home for a Bible study. The chief then informed me there was a felony warrant out for Tim's arrest for assault. I asked if I was expected to arrest Tim when he showed up at my house. The chief thought about this and said no, because that would be like arresting a person in church. You just don't do that.

I lived about midway down a hill on a dead-end street. I asked, in a rather snippy tone, if he was going to have on-duty officers waiting for Tim to arrest him as he left the study. The chief said he would put out an order not to touch Tim for two hours after the study concluded. He then proceeded to tell me that he didn't understand my relationship to these kids. He went on to say he had tried to get a city ordinance passed about assemblage on Mill Street at the time I started the Bible study. But because the kids were no longer meeting there, the ordinance failed. He was both baffled and somewhat angry about this.

That evening Tim showed for the Bible study. I told him of the warrant and suggested that after the Bible study he should turn himself in to the officers on duty. He did. Now the practical theology came into play.

Tim was booked into the Hennepin County Jail that evening. He went in the next morning for arraignment. Bail was set at four thousand dollars. Tim's friends came to me and asked if I could help them with the bail money. I told them I was walking a very fine line by entertaining felons in my home, and because of this, I could not. I still had city and departmental policy to deal with. They asked how they were going to raise the money to get him out of jail. I reminded them we had been studying about trusting God, and we should wait and see what God was going to do.

Tim had to go back into court, and when the judge found out that he had no permanent address, he raised the bail to six thousand dollars. These kids really became unglued and asked, "What is God doing?" I told them to keep praying and watching.

The following day I went to see Tim in jail. Because I carried a badge, I had no problem getting in to see him. We talked and I asked if there was anything he needed. He told me he had his Bible and that was really all he needed. He told me that being in jail was giving him plenty of time to read and study. He went on to tell me that he would be at Bible study Thursday night. He said he wasn't sure how, but he was sure he would be there.

The following day Tim met with his public defender. Tim told him how he had been attending this Bible study and how he really wanted to be there on Thursday night. The public defender went to the judge and told him Tim had been attending a Bible study at a cop's home, and he would like to attend, as they were really into some interesting stuff. The judge released Tim with no bail. He was what we called RPR'd (Released on Personal Recognizance). It was late Thursday afternoon when Tim was released.

The Bible study had already started when there was a knock at the back door. A girl opened the door and then slammed it shut. She yelled, "It's Tim!" I told her to let him in. Tim had quite a testimony as to what had happened and it was a faith builder that night for all of the kids. I read to them a similar story about Peter in the book of Acts, and how an angel of the Lord had released the apostle Peter from prison.

> So Peter was kept in the prison, but prayer for him was being made fervently by the church to God. And on the very night when Herod was about to bring him forward, Peter was sleeping between two soldiers, bound with two chains; and guards in front of the door were watching over the prison. And behold, an angel of the Lord suddenly

appeared, and a light shone in the cell; and he struck Peter's side and roused him, saying, "Get up quickly." And his chains fell off his hands. And the angel said to him, "Gird yourself and put on your sandals." And he did so. And he said to him, "Wrap your cloak around you and follow me." And he went out and continued to follow, and he did not know that what was being done by the angel was real, but thought he was seeing a vision. And when they had passed the first and second guard, they came to the iron gate that leads into the city, which opened for them by itself; and they went out and went along one street; and immediately the angel departed from him. And when Peter came to himself, he said, "Now I know for sure that the Lord has sent forth His angel and rescued me from the hand of Herod and from all that the Jewish people were expecting." And when he realized this, he went to the house of Mary, the mother of John who was also called Mark, where many were gathered together and were praying. And when he knocked at the door of the gate, a servant-girl named Rhoda came to answer. And when she recognized Peter's voice, because of her joy she did not open the gate, but ran in and announced that Peter was standing in front of the gate. And they said to her, "You are out of your mind!" But she kept insisting that it was so. And they kept saying, "It is his angel." But Peter continued knocking; and when they had opened the door, they saw him and were amazed. But motioning to them with his hand to be silent, he described to them how the Lord had led him out of the prison. And he said, "Report these things to James and the brethren." And he departed and went to another place.

—Acts 12:5-17 (NASB)

As far as these kids were concerned, this was the book of Acts come alive in practice that day. News of this spread on the street, and the number of kids attending the Bible study grew. As I stated earlier, there were some forty kids regularly attending by the time we closed the study down.

Wrap Up

In 1980 the police chief that hired me retired. The new police chief and I did not get along well. After he had been with our department for a year, he instituted annual reviews. During the first review, he informed me that he highly doubted whether I had the ability or aptitude to be a police officer. I told him he was entitled to his opinion.

The form we had to sign, indicating that the review had been held, also contained a number of questions at the end of it. It was something along the lines of, "What is your motivation in doing the job the way you do?" Boy, did he open the door on that one. I wrote, "He has told you, O man, what is good; And what does the Lord require of you But to do justice, to love kindness, And to walk humbly with your God?" (Micah 6:8 NASB). I then wrote, "Thank you for asking."

I signed the review and gave it back to the chief. He was somewhat disturbed over my response and in a raised voice asked, "Don't you realize that I have to show this to the city manager?" I told him I did and left it at that.

It was shortly after this when I left the Wayzata Police Department and was hired by the Orono Police Department. The Wayzata chief held a going-away party for me. Personally, I believe he was happy to see me go. The party was unadvertised, and at the gathering he said that if I were retiring from law enforcement, he would probably have to rent the Minneapolis Auditorium to accommodate all the people because of the large number of lives I had touched since joining the Wayzata Police Department. Since I was only going to another department, he saw no need for that. He did want my list of confidential, reliable informants. No one knew who my informants were except me, and no one ever received such a list from me.

Within the first few months of joining the Orono Police Department, I was involved in three shootings. After the last situation, the Orono chief commented, "Bet you thought you were coming to a quiet department." In all my years in law enforcement, I was the target in about ten shootings or attempted knifings, both on and off duty. Most are documented, but not all. I simply did not see the need to document them at the time.

I only fired my weapon once on the street in fifteen years. That one shot cost me thirty-three pages of paperwork. A suspect was trying to lead me into an ambush after using a sledge hammer to destroy my squad car.

One of my duties with the Orono Police Department was to train a S.W.A.T. team (Special Weapons and Tactics). The chief came to me one day and stated that because of my military background and the fact that I had seen combat, he wanted me to train a tactical team and teach those young officers how to stay alive. I accepted the challenge.

We had an interesting group of officers who wanted to be a part of the team. There were a total of eight on the team and everyone had a nickname. Mine was given to me by the assistant police chief. I was called "Rabbi." It was meant as a slam, but I thanked him for it. I asked if he knew what Rabbi meant, and of course he didn't. I told him it meant "Teacher," and since I was the instructor, it fit.

The team leader was "War Lord" and the youngest member was "Puddles." One of the officers had his own arsenal, including an AR-15, a .223 varmint rifle with scope, and shotguns and they all had names. One of the other guys had an Uzi (semi-automatic, 9mm, Israeli manufactured). I have to admit we became a very good S.W.A.T. team. We logged seven call-outs without ever firing a shot. All the situations were resolved peacefully.

The team leader wanted me on the entry team. He noticed that during practices I always knew (or seemed to know) what the interior of the buildings looked like. Also, he felt I was "tight with God," and with me as the shield, no one else would get hurt. Just as a humorous aside, one night when I was not on duty, a group of officers had just cleared a situation and were standing by their cars talking about it. All of a sudden there was a bolt of lightening with a loud boom after it. They ducked instinctively. After they laughed about it for a moment, one asked, "Where's Griffiths?" They claimed they really thought I had something to do with this.

After receiving the nickname of Rabbi, a Jewish friend of mine got me a yarmulke from his temple and gave it to me. I would wear this from time to time around the squad room and this drove my sergeant up a wall. We had fun, but we got the job done.

In my lifetime I have seen much excitement and a lot of death and tragedy. I have also witnessed the hand of God moving in and through me in mighty ways. Previously I asked my readers, "Have you ever wondered what it would be like to be used by God in a miraculous way?" As I have written this book and recounted numerous events, I have asked the Lord to speak to readers in such a fashion that they would desire to seek Him and allow Him to work through their lives. With that in mind, I would be remiss not to include one last chapter on how to obtain this power.

CHAPTER NINE

HOW TO OBTAIN
THIS POWER

IN CHAPTER THREE I wrote of my conversion experience. I am not about to tell anyone that if they did not hear bells, see visions, or *feel* anything, that they did not have a true conversion experience. As the old expression goes, "The proof of the pudding is in the eating." Or, staying scriptural, "So then, you will know them by their fruits" (Matthew 7:20 NASB). So it is with one's conversion. When it comes to things of the Spirit, one must go by faith, not by sight or the senses.

A friend of mine wrote a short little chorus back in the 1970's entitled "Go By Faith, Not By Sight." The last line of the chorus is "Oh blessed are they who receive, yet have not seen you." You may not feel anything at conversion, but you will see a change in your life. Simply ask God to forgive you of all the times you have fallen short and sinned.

> For all have sinned and fall short of the glory of God.
>
> —Romans 3:23 (NASB)

> Repent therefore and return, that your sins may be wiped away, in order that times of refreshing may come from the presence of the Lord.
>
> —Acts 3:19 (NASB)

> As far as the east is from the west, so far has He removed our transgressions from us.
>
> —Psalm 103:12 (NASB)

Ask Jesus to come into your life, and then surrender your life to Him. If it sounds really simple, it is. There is no other way to get to know God on a personal basis. Remember that Jesus said, "I am the way, and the truth, and the life; no one comes to the Father, but through Me" (John 14:6 NASB).

Some would say that this is very narrow thinking. Yet these are the instructions for salvation. To phone a friend, one cannot dial just any phone number; there is a particular phone number that has been assigned to the friend. Now *that* is narrow thinking. There is only one way to God the Father, and that is through His Son, Jesus Christ.

After you have asked Jesus to come into your life, ask Him to fill you with His Holy Spirit. Then watch what the Lord will do through you. The job of the Holy Spirit is to lift up the name of Jesus. I have heard it said that one has as much of the Holy Spirit as one is going to get when one receives Christ. This is true, but the more we surrender our lives to the Lord, the more of Him will be seen in us. The Scriptures will come alive in and around us, and the more exciting this life in the Holy Spirit becomes. Serving the Lord and allowing Him to rule and reign in our lives is a daily process. No life could be more satisfying and exciting than the one turned over to Jesus

> The thief comes only to steal, and kill, and destroy; I came that they might have life, and might have it abundantly.
>
> —John 10:10 (NASB)

There are different Greek words meaning power. One is *exousia*, which means authority, right, and strength. This is the giving of authoritative power by God. He loves us that much that He is willing to give us that power.

> But as many as received him, to them gave he power to become the sons of God, even to them that believe on his name.
>
> —John 1:12 (KJV)

We receive the *exousia* in becoming a child of God.

Another word for power is *dunamis,* which is demonstrated power such as in a dynamo generating electricity, or the effects of dynamite being exploded.

> But ye shall receive power, after that the Holy Ghost is come upon you: and ye shall be witnesses unto me both in Jerusalem, and in all Judaea, and in Samaria, and unto the uttermost part of the earth.
>
> —Acts 1:8 (KJV)

This verse says that we shall receive power (*dunamis*) after the Holy Spirit is upon us. For what reason do we receive this power? So we may become witnesses of Jesus to the "uttermost part of the earth."

The form of *dunamis* is not available without first receiving *exousia.* One must first receive Jesus as Savior and as Lord, and in doing so, become a child of God.

> For all who are being led by the Spirit of God, these are sons of God. For you have not received a spirit of slavery leading to fear again, but you have received a spirit of adoption as sons by which we cry out, "Abba! Father!" The Spirit Himself bears witness with our spirit that we are children of God, and if children, heirs also, heirs of God and fellow heirs with Christ, if indeed we suffer with Him in order that we may also be glorified with Him.
>
> —Romans 8:14-17 (NASB)

After the command to become children of God, we then have the command to be filled with the Holy Spirit. This means we first receive the *exousia,* and then we receive the *dunamis.* Both are power, but one gives the authority to be used by the other.

"And they went forth, and preached every where, the Lord working with them, and confirming the word with signs following" (Mark 16:20 KJV). The disciples were sent out to preach salvation. What impresses me is that this verse says the Lord worked *with* them. It sums up my life in Christ Jesus. As I have ministered both on and off the job, the Lord has continuously worked through me for His glory. To God be the glory, great things He has done.

Now to Him who is able to keep you from stumbling, and to make you stand in the presence of His glory blameless with great joy, to the only God our Savior, through Jesus Christ our Lord, be glory, majesty, dominion and authority, before all time and now and forever. Amen.

—Jude 24-25 (NASB)

ENDNOTES

1. C. Peter Wagner, *Your Spiritual Gifts Can Help Your Church Grow,* (Regal Books- 1979) 102

2. Ibid. 228

3. *The Wind Is Alive,* LP Record, Jesus People Music, 1979, (60 min)

4. Ibid, 237

5. The Sharrett Brothers, *I Am Willing Lord,* LP Record, Word Records, 1976, (34 min)

PW

To order additional copies of this book call:
1-877-421-READ (7323)
or please visit our Web site at
www.pleasantwordbooks.com

If you enjoyed this quality custom-published book,
drop by our Web site for more books and information.

www.winepressgroup.com
"Your partner in custom publishing."

Breinigsville, PA USA
26 July 2010
242407BV00002B/2/P

9 781414 116006